"Finally! A unique guide to cultivating a vibrant, healthy marriage. Readers will be captivated by the mystic world of a Navy SEAL. This book allows the reader a glimpse of what these warriors face and how they come out on top on the battlefield and in life. With a sense of humility, Laviolette does an outstanding job of weaving his military experiences to these time-worn interpersonal principles."

—Dr. Anthony J. Castro
Clinical Psychologist
Author, *Creating Space for Happiness:*
The Secret of Giving Room

"I've been a pastor and army chaplain for thirty years. Darek has packed a grad-school course in psychology and Gary Chapman's The Five Love Languages *into one intense book. I've deployed to Iraq three times. I've watched countless military marriages flounder and fail. In every case, the couple did not have the skills and self-awareness needed to do the hard work to make their marriage thrive. Darek Laviolette's gut-honest testimony to his failure in his marriage is filled with practical, clear guidance to wives who are married to military members. It is a wake-up call to elite warriors and military members of all stripes. It is a clarion call to military couples drifting toward divorce. It guides the reader to self-awareness and growth while laying out a defined path to building what every military couple wants: a healthy, vibrant, growing marriage."*

—Chaplain (Colonel) John Morris
United States Army

"After twenty-four years in 'that man's army' as a controller, instructor, supply warrant officer, and finally helicopter warrant officer and having endured a most painful and unexpected divorce and having been raised in a similar environment to that of Darek's, I can genuinely relate to almost every aspect of his book.

His profound insight into couples' backgrounds is the same thing we pilots learn about in Crew Resource Management (CRM) in understanding how to play and work well with others, especially when unbeknownst to us, other pilots bring not only their stick and rudder skills to the cockpit . . . they bring their entire families, their latest family frustrations, and their entire upbringings!

I am quite impressed with Darek's candor and sincerity, high intelligence, and most of all, his great ability to simplify complex entities—seemingly intangible notions and feelings—into concrete, understandable, and reasonable analogies.

I learned much and realized things I already had ideas about from his book, with eternal questions like 'Why did my husband leave me?' and 'Why did my marriage fail?' Even though I was divorced nearly twenty years ago, it still causes me great pain.

Now, I feel I should send this book to my ex-husband, along with an apology! This book is a must read not only for couples in chaos and unhappiness, not only for military couples enduring 'yo-yo,' relationships, but for all couples—especially those just beginning."

—Terry Ann Salazar
Med; Retired Senior Captain
CW4, US Army

"I thoroughly enjoyed reading this book. I felt understood— someone finally gets it!

A S.E.A.L. to Heal Your Marriage *is a great source of information and an effective tool if you are serious about the search for healing. It is about more than just marriage and relationships; it goes deeper, to the core of self-discovery. It is a wonderful guide in the journey to find who you are, your purpose, and your roles and responsibilities in life. The book is a very enlightening read but also contains compelling stories of life in the elite Navy SEALs and, most importantly, true stories of love, marriage, and family.*

Darek pours his soul into this book and exposes key pitfalls to avoid. If you seriously desire to become the person you want to be concerning your marriage and family, this is a must read! Definitely a best seller in the making!

—Marcia Ardito
Sales Representative, Black Pearl Source

A S.E.A.L. TO HEAL

YOUR MARRIAGE

A S.E.A.L. TO HEAL YOUR MARRIAGE

A Decorated Navy SEAL's Operational Guide
to Heal Your Relationship

DAREK LAVIOLETTE

Advantage®

Published by Advantage, Charleston, South Carolina.
Member of Advantage Media Group.

ADVANTAGE is a registered trademark, and the Advantage colophon is a trademark of Advantage Media Group, Inc.

Printed in the United States of America.

ISBN: 978-1-59932-692-4
LCCN: 2016938624

Tree Neutral

Advantage Media Group is proud to be a part of the Tree Neutral® program. Tree Neutral offsets the number of trees consumed in the production and printing of this book by taking proactive steps such as planting trees in direct proportion to the number of trees used to print books. To learn more about Tree Neutral, please visit **www.treeneutral.com.** To learn more about Advantage's commitment to being a responsible steward of the environment, please visit **www.advantagefamily.com/green**

Advantage Media Group is a publisher of business, self-improvement, and professional development books and online learning. We help entrepreneurs, business leaders, and professionals share their Stories, Passion, and Knowledge to help others Learn & Grow. Do you have a manuscript or book idea that you would like us to consider for publishing? Please visit **advantagefamily.com** or call **1.866.775.1696.**

To Sam and my children

TABLE OF CONTENTS

Conclusion:

FOREWORD

Key missions often require Special Forces to be a success, Special Forces like the Navy SEALs.

When the stakes are high enough, we call upon the world's most elite soldiers. They have turned the tides in conflicts all over the globe and made the key difference in operations we'll never know about.

These are the soldiers Darek fought beside and even trained. But when it comes to marriage and family, the stakes couldn't be any higher.

Broken homes and broken lives are the root of so much pain, with hurting people hurting other people. Besides the impact to society, our individual health, our family's health, and freedom are the stakes in this conflict. Recent, in-depth studies have shown that the single greatest factor in human happiness is positive social connections. In a 2015 TED talk, Robert Waldinger, an American psychiatrist and professor at Harvard Medical School, concluded that "the good life is built with good relationships." But we don't need a Harvard professor's research to know it's the truth. The vast majority of humans know this intuitively and from life experience. We are built to be connected, and the consequences of negative relationships are on par with the immense benefits of positive ones.

In 2012, while on the brink of a nearly finalized divorce, I came to know Mr. Laviolette through the online course on marriage called EC (Environment Changers). Bound by a common mission to mend broken families, the men and women in EC are some of the most courageous, authentic, and genuinely good people I've ever known. With so much personal gratitude and respect for the SEALs, I felt honored to have an opportunity to talk with Darek throughout the course. My father is a Navy veteran, along with the many other veterans in my family, which gave me a deep appreciation for all men and women who serve in the armed forces.

Thanks to the drastic personal changes that developed from what I learned in the course, lots of faith, and a phenomenal wife, I was able to join in on the success stories by saving a marriage that was on the verge of divorce. But I quickly learned that there was much more work to be done to rebuild. Darek teamed up with me and became an integral part of the success I now enjoy with my family. With laser focus, determination, and inspiration, we decided to take on everything in our lives that did not serve us or anyone else.

After months of facing battle after battle—internal and external—I started to get discouraged. Darek shared, "The work I've done on relationships is harder than anything I've done in the SEAL teams." Understanding the significance of that statement, I was very humbled and encouraged. Through further studies, talks, and trial and error, we found clarity. We uncovered answers, and gained a better understanding of ourselves, the women in our lives, our unique families, and our universe. By applying the principles and wisdom we've gained to achieve emotional control, we found more and more success in all our relationships.

Together we first learned of Dr. Hew Len and ho'oponopono, and we had the opportunity to attend his workshops in our respective cities, within weeks of each other. Since we were the only ECs to attend the ho'oponopono workshop (at that time), we worked through what we learned and experienced to better apply it to our lives. No topic was off-limits in our quest for healing and reconciliation of our families. This was a spiritual journey of epic proportions, and we couldn't be any more determined. But the journey was not without perils along the way. Tackling twenty-plus years of clinical depression and estranged family is a dangerous proposition. Quite literally, Darek had to talk me off the ledge more than once, as I faced some of the greatest challenges in my life. By choosing to take 100 percent responsibility for everything in our awareness, we proceeded to address all relationship issues by looking in the mirror first. The only person we have true control over is ourselves. So we decided to change ourselves instead of demanding or expecting others to change.

With depression, I've lost many friends and baffled many mental-health professionals. Most would not dare venture into the emotional depths to discover the root. But Darek did. He was the only one with the courage to stand and face this challenge, seeing it through to the end. With Darek's support, I turned the corner on decades of depression and began winning in my mind and family! With immense gratitude, I told Darek, "It literally took a SEAL to heal this!"

———

You now have an opportunity to learn the same proven strategies and principles. By applying the wealth of international knowledge and experience of a Navy SEAL trainer, this book provides a solid foundation to build great relationships, which equal great marriages and great lives. Prepare to be challenged, enlightened, encouraged, validated, empowered, equipped, and healed by the pages that follow.

This operational guide is tried-and-true, tested by fire. It prepares you for one of the greatest missions and epic battles of all time: the battle for yourself and your family—a battle that requires the most elite Special Forces training to answer the call. This is an ultra high-stakes mission with impacts for generations and countless people.

It's time to "man-up" and be the best "you" that's possible. Utilize the Reconnaissance and High-Resolution Intelligence, follow your Execution Orders, and achieve Mission Success! This operational guide provides everything you need to be successful. Be the man you're designed to be through the immeasurable power of love—the greatest healing force in the universe.

—Brian G. Patridge

PREFACE

TO THE WIVES OF THE MEN I WROTE THIS BOOK FOR

This book began as an apology to my ex-wife. In turning my "I'm sorry" into a book, I hope to provide you with an operational guide to save your broken marriage.

I wish I wasn't reaching you at this late date.

As a wife, you believed that long-told lie that you could fall in love with some guy, and your love would become a magical bubble, protecting you both from harm. The reverse is true. Love is fragile—it's the thing that needs protection. If you are considering giving this book to your husband, as I suggest, that means you have followed the lie about love all the way to the end.

In one way, leaving your husband makes sense. At this point, it might be the only thing that gets his attention. As I explain to men in this book, after they get married, they begin treating their wives as their dads treated the women they'd married. It's programmed into them. But you wanted to marry the man you fell in love with . . . not his father!

This is why I suggest that you send your husband this book, with or without an explanation. It will get his attention, and who knows, he might even read it. I'm a Navy SEAL. I've worked with men under all kinds of conditions, and using that experience and the failure of my own marriage, I will explain to your guy how and why your relationship collapsed. If he's like most men, he doesn't know the reasons, and he really needs to.

When a woman rejects her intimate relationship through divorce, it's the most devastating thing she can do to her man, and yet it might be the only thing that wakes him up from his deep sleep. So send this book off, and let your husband and me do the rest. Maybe you're hoping that it's not too late for your marriage and that, with the right advice, your husband can change. You might be sending it to him because you still want him to have a good life, or perhaps you simply want to know that he finally listened to your concerns. Whatever the case, send him a copy of *A S.E.A.L. to Heal Your Marriage*. It will make you feel good about you.

—Darek Laviolette

ACKNOWLEDGMENTS

There are many people who deserve to be acknowledged for their presence, influence, or direct contribution for helping me discover the reason why success in my most personal relationships is possible and so rewarding to finally find. It is no small irony that I have found purpose in being able to expose my failures in marriage in a way that helps you, dear reader, to keep what is most important.

I want to start by thanking my parents, Anne and Chuck Laviolette. I wouldn't *be* if it wasn't for them, and how do I know whether I wasn't supposed to have the terrible relationship programming I got from them? It was from that programming that I was able to lose everything and yet still have the grit to face my unexpected lot in life head on—and in a way that truly touches hearts. My parents are my essence, and if I reject them, then I reject parts of me. It's much nicer on the heart to love all of me. So, Mom, Dad—thank you for being exactly who you are. Thank you for giving me the iron will to survive and thrive despite any situation I've encountered. Thank you for everything. I love you very much.

The next thank-you goes to Larry Bilotta and Life Discoveries, Inc. After my marriage collapsed, I didn't have anywhere else to turn. If it wasn't for the things I learned with Life Discoveries, I wouldn't have the optimism and faith that marriage can still be absolute bliss, even if mine had ended. Larry, you were the father figure I needed at that time in my life to teach what my dad wasn't put here to do for me. You were the doctor who kept me alive when I didn't see a whole lot of reason to want to continue. I thank you personally for what you have done in my life regularly. You always tell me that I have your beautiful wife, Marsha, to thank for any insight you have been able to share with me over the years. So this is my public thank-you to you and your beautiful bride for providing such a reliable and supportive backstop for me to grow and to then be trusted to reach out to the world with the Life Discoveries message of real hope for those who are desperate to save their marriages. I appreciate you both greatly. Thank you so much for all of your support.

The group of men and women who have come together to fight for their families under the Life Discoveries banner also deserve to be mentioned. The Environment Changers, Bill Wolf, Andrew Evans, Clint Howell, Don Taubin, Clay Beale, Bob Trembly, Matt Finn, Snookie, Stephanie Mehring, and a special thank-you to Brian Patridge who has spent countless hours working through all kinds of good things to find bliss that is hard to imagine. Thanks, bud.

There are people who shared their stories in this book, who allowed me to share their story but wish to remain anonymous because they are still operational. I thank them for winning in their marriages when it seemed easier at some times to relent. I greatly appreciate you trusting in my words and your courage to do what most can't or won't. A big thank-you to Professor Tim Adams, who helped start me on the process to write this book.

An additional thank-you to everyone at Advantage Media Group. Barry Pearce, thank you for your amazing writing expertise and time. I greatly appreciate you, bud. Eland Mann, Helen Harris, Alison Morse, George Stevens, Elise Nissen, and the rest of the Advantage Team—your dedication to your clients is amazing, and I greatly appreciate the time and professionalism you put into helping me deliver this elaborate operational guide and apology to my ex-wife and children. Thank you for believing in me and for your guidance.

Last but certainly not least: as Larry Bilotta tells me that it is Marsha who deserves the thanks for the impact she has made, this thank-you is to Sam—my amazing first wife, the beautiful mother of our two incredible children. If you had not done what you did when you did, I would be a hopelessly lost soul still wondering what I was supposed to be doing on this planet. Sam, the loss I endured has become a great gain for me and many other people. Your impact in my life saves marriages and families every day. You taught me how important it is to look at the world from a lens bigger than the very small, screwed-up one I showed up with. You have forced me to become the man I always wanted to be, and I appreciate you more than words will ever be able to tell. I love you, Sam. Thank you so very much for everything.

INTRODUCTION

I n 2002, I had the world by the tail.

I was a twenty-nine-year-old Navy SEAL at the height of my career. After eleven years in the navy, I was heading to the Naval Special Warfare Development Group. A lot of people still know NSWDG as "SEAL Team Six" (the name of its predecessor). It's a Special Mission Unit that falls under the Joint Special Operations Command, the counterpart of the Army's Delta Force. I was headed for an elite job with one of the most elite fighting forces in the world. Everything was going my way professionally.

And personally.

I had a beautiful Australian wife and a two-year-old son, I had learned Arabic at the Defense Language Institute, and I was finishing up orders in Bahrain.

I had met my wife, Samantha, while on a deployment to the Middle East in 1997. Sam had gone there to be with her father, an advertising executive who had work in the region. She was a former Pan American swimmer, and while in the Persian Gulf, she began teaching swimming to ultra-wealthy clients. She was gorgeous, athletic, and organized, and she made more money as a swimming teacher than I did as a SEAL. Sam was smart and the sweetest, most loving person I'd ever met.

It was the kind of intense romance you read about, the kind everybody hopes for. We were engaged in three months and then married by a justice of the peace six months later in San Diego. Six months after that, we went down to Australia for the official wedding. The way I saw it, there was not a guy on the planet who did not want to be me.

After we got married, Sam and I lived near Coronado, CA, home of SEAL training and a stunning resort town close to San Diego. After that, we went to Monterey for my intensive language training, and then from there to Bahrain for two years, where we lived in the house of the former naval attaché for the British embassy, a palatial home in a walled compound. It was fantastic.

Our son was two, and our daughter was born after I was sent to NSWDG—two beautiful, healthy kids.

Samantha was a wonderful wife and mother. She is one of the most efficient and organized people I have ever met. Anyone who walked into our home immediately felt welcome. Everything was immaculate. She has a gift for listening and is incredibly loving. Her reaction to just about anyone who showed up in her life seemed to be, "I really love listening to them." We moved a lot because of my job—San Diego, Monterey, Bahrain, Virginia, San Diego, and Chicago. Sam would have rather stayed put when we got to Virginia, but she also liked to travel and made the best of those difficult transitions.

Everything was going well, yet something wasn't right. I could never quite put my finger on what was wrong. My entire life had been like that. With so much good on the surface, I did not understand why things were as hard as they were. I did not understand why my mom was the way she was. I did not understand why my wife was the way she was.

Most of all, I did not understand why I was the way I was.

Despite everything positive, I was discontented. I was unhappy about a lot of things that I wasn't getting as a man. I wasn't happy about my parents and their interactions with my family and me. I wasn't happy with Sam; we started fighting all the time. I was going down the Navy SEAL road and getting accolades and respect and doing exactly what a SEAL should do, but I did not feel fulfilled.

For some reason, I couldn't get along. I couldn't play well with others. What do I mean? Here's a typical example.

Sam and I were both swimmers growing up. I'm a great athlete, and so is she. We decided to go running together. Sounds good, right—a nice opportunity to do something healthy and fun while bonding with your spouse? Well, not with me on board. While we ran, I started giving her this critique of her running style: *You should run like this,* or *You are doing that wrong, it would be more efficient if you* . . . Get the picture? She's just going for a run with me because she's a cool lady, and I turn it into a disaster by analyzing everything she does. My intentions were great, but it became pure criticism and no fun at all.

I realize now that I did this with basically every aspect of her life. It didn't matter how many different ways Sam stood on her head to try to please me; she was never going to be successful in trying to do so—because I wasn't pleased with myself. I wasn't pleased or fulfilled or happy, even though all these other great things were happening for me and even though many guys would have gladly taken my place.

Sam tried to keep the peace—that's her M.O.—but she resented me, and it began to show. I resented her, too. I was working hard and gone a lot, and when I came home, I wanted to fall immediately back into the role of dad and husband, to raise my kids and be close to my wife. But she treated my interactions with the kids as intrusive and kept me at arm's length. I wasn't getting the intimacy I needed at home, so I began getting it elsewhere. Of course, this only increased the tension, and I felt guilty as hell. Mine was a life full of infidelity, argument, and grief. This was not how things were supposed to go, and I couldn't even explain to myself how it all happened.

In 2003, deployed in Afghanistan, I had an experience on a mountaintop that brought me face-to-face with my mortality. I decided to turn over a new leaf and get my marriage back on track. I

This was not how things were supposed to go, and I couldn't even explain to myself how it all happened.

vowed that I would be a good husband and father. I stopped cheating and started going to church. I tried to get Sam involved in my revived interest in religion. We went to see a psychologist. We tried counseling and therapy. Nothing worked—at least, not for long. We still argued all the time—about money, religion, the kids, you name it.

She went back to Australia in 2008, and in 2010, Sam and I officially got divorced.

I think of myself as a good person . . . don't we all? I wanted to do right by my wife and kids. I wanted to make them happy, and I wanted to be happy. So why was it all so hard? I am a Navy SEAL. I'm disciplined and resourceful, and once I have a goal, I do everything I can to achieve it. But this goal eluded me. No matter how hard I tried, I could not seem to clean up the mess. I couldn't even articulate what the mess was, how things had gotten so bad, or what was really causing our problems.

The epiphany I had on that mountaintop in Afghanistan turned out to be the start of a long, arduous journey. I spent the next decade searching and reflecting, trying to understand how things had gone wrong. What I didn't know was that this would mean exploring in depth why Sam and I were the way we were, how we'd gotten there, and even how our parents and their parents had developed into the people they were.

I read many important books along the way. In particular, courses offered by Larry Bilotta of Life Discoveries, Inc. were key to my learning what I never knew about marriage and relationships. It was these courses that allowed me to understand the dynamics that had doomed my marriage from the very beginning and, more important, all the mistakes I could have avoided.

For instance, I grew up with parents who wanted virtually everything to be better. That's why I always found something to complain about. I was programmed to improve everything, and that included my wife, no matter how good she was. It all played out in my marriage. I was given an angel, and I criticized the hell out of the angel until she had to leave. I was oblivious to this at the time because I didn't understand the way programs repeat in us from one generation to another.

Our childhood "programming" is made up of the attitudes, beliefs, and ways of interacting that we observed in our parents during our first ten years of life. As Sam and I embarked on the process of learning about this dynamic, I felt like I was getting introduced to my wife for the first time. I slowly began to understand her programming and mine, along with all the actions and attitudes I had been dumping on her.

All those times I'd come home after being away for work, I wanted immediate intimacy. I never understood that I was creating our lack of connection. There were many things, large and small, that I wasn't doing that would have created a connection with Sam— accepting people as they were, adopting a live-and-let-live heart and mind, helping out around the house, helping with the kids, and relieving her burdens. These were all things she might have appreciated. I wasn't making my wife's life a song or letting her know I understood that it was worthwhile to romance her. (Translation for guys: I wasn't leaving space for foreplay—not sexual foreplay, but the little things that were meaningful to her. Believe it or not, if your marriage is in shambles and you are not getting sexual intimacy, she doesn't want to hear you crying about it. She wants romance and to feel cherished, and you dropped that ball. It's up to you to pick that ball up again with vigor. And meanwhile, drop the requirement for her to want to come through for you on that front.)

A lot of guys reading this are in the same boat with their own wives and girlfriends, whether they know it or not. If you're at the point where a woman doesn't seem to want to have sex with you anymore, it's not because you're suddenly undesirable, but it's probably because they're not getting their own needs met. Whether they know it consciously or not, they're thinking, *I have no reason to have sex with this guy.*

I came to realize with Sam that I had been treating her the way that *I* want to be treated. I was not treating her the way *she* wanted to be treated, a way that would make her feel loved and cared for. I was married to her for eight years before I saw what she needed, and in the entire time of our marriage, I showed her that I really loved her fewer than five times.

How can a man go a year, or even several, without showing his wife that he loves her? It's easier than you think, and if your marriage or relationship isn't going well, odds are good that your lady feels neglected. Remember, it was not that I didn't want to show my wife I loved her. My intentions were good, but I just didn't understand her needs. I was attempting to show her "love" in the ways *I* wanted to be loved, not in the ways that would have meant the most to her. This is one of the glaring problems in troubled marriages.

If you will allow me, I will show you how to avoid the mistakes I made and give you the simple tools, developed over many years, to build a successful relationship or restore a troubled one. In these pages, I will offer a working understanding of why we do the things we do and why our spouses act the way they do in marriage. This book will help you get relationships right for yourself and for those you love. It will allow you to stop potential problems in their tracks. If you have negative momentum that's already pushing you and your partner in the wrong direction, then this book offers a way to say, "We're going to make child's play of these issues." I'll show you how to do this by truly seeing the solutions to the problems and taking a better path.

> I was attempting to show her "love" in the ways *I* wanted to be loved, not in the ways that would have meant the most to her.

OPERATIONAL TERMINOLOGY TO HEAL YOUR MARRIAGE

Navy SEALs approach missions in a particular way—a disciplined, determined way that guarantees the best chance of success. This is the unique approach I'm offering you for restoring or improving your marriage. Just as if you were a SEAL embarking on the mission of a lifetime, I'll give you a **Target Package** that includes **High-Resolution Intelligence** on yourself and your spouse and essential environmental data (emotional, historical, intellectual, etc.) that's vital to **Mission Success**. This information will be used to complete an **Actions-On Plan** with **Execution Orders**. You will refine the plan as you gain insight by conducting additional **Reconnaissance**. This is the groundwork you need to engage in **Direct-Action Operations** that will provide you and your spouse with the best chance of marital success.

Throughout the book, these operational terms will serve as resources to help you heal your marriage:

- **Target Package** = A big-picture view of all the intelligence you need to discover your relationship's true who, what, why, where, and how—before it self-destructs on your watch.

- **High-Resolution Intelligence** = Examples, lessons, and stories from my life and the lives of others that you can use to save your relationship.

- **Reconnaissance** = Professional help, giving you insight on the enemy inside of you. (But remember—don't focus on the enemy. Focus clearly on your beautiful wife.) Use these professional tools to learn to look beyond your bad side that's destroying your marriage.

- **Actions-On Plan** = The development phase. Using intelligence to prep for mission. Applying the information you've learned by imagining and planning in your head and heart.

- **Direct-Action Operations** = Being engaged with your spouse. This could mean actively letting conflict happen—and keeping your cool. Choosing to not allow yourself to resort to conflict. Healing the old ways. Understand her, don't fight back, and allow negative energy to dissipate. This means being bulletproof. Whatever she throws at you, you accept it, take responsibility for it, and return only love. She's beautiful, and she's worth it, and you're going to get it right.

- **Execution Orders** = Implementing the plan. Your execution orders come at each chapter's conclusion.

- **Mission Success** = Healing your marriage. Winning in love.

You didn't get married because you wanted to get divorced, and you certainly aren't staying married and miserable because you want to live that way. War is hell, and love is war. This book is predicated on the idea that winning in love requires the same training, intelligence, discipline, and commitment that soldiers need to defeat a ruthless enemy. And your enemy is not in her—*it's in you.*

In the most civil relationship circumstances, I'd recommend that both partners read this book, but *it only takes one.* If you are the one who decides to take 100 percent responsibility for your life, including your relationship, then you can heal it without your wife helping in any way. The misstep most men make is attempting to mend a troubled marriage by laboring under the delusion that their wife has problems that must be "fixed." As I'll explain in the following pages, this approach puts you in the position of either becoming a doormat or a tyrant, and either way, you are destined to fail.

> War is hell, and love is war. And your enemy is not in her—*it's in you.*

Instead, I'll help you understand the workings of your relationship, the sources of friction, and the things you can do on your own to completely change what's going on between you. Of course, the process takes focus, and good results can appear suddenly, but it typically takes some time to see steady results. The longer you demand help and support from your wife, the longer this will take. I'll say it again: *it only takes one to heal a marriage.* Two people who both take 100 percent responsibility for their own emotions, beliefs, attitudes, and actions could have a relationship that everyone would envy, but that rarely happens. I'm encouraging you to be the one who gets it done.

In the following chapters, I'll explore these concepts in depth:

- **Awakening.** This means understanding the ways that you become the problem in your marriage and how you can transform into the solution on your own. Unlike many books, classes, and therapy methods, *A S.E.A.L. to Heal Your Marriage* requires only *one* partner to make it work. Learn the steps a man can take on his own to create what he's wanted all along—a relationship where he loves and is loved in return.

- **The real Golden Rule.** Most of us were taught to treat others as we wish to be treated. Sounds nice, but it's disastrous in relationships. I'll teach you how to apply the real Golden Rule: treat others as *they* wish to be treated.

- **Patterns of life.** Women are programmed by their mothers in how to treat a man. During their first ten years, little girls get the "how-to" placed in their brains by watching the way Mom treats Dad. Men are programmed by their fathers in how to treat a woman. They get that info in their brains by watching how Dad treats Mom. Consequently, by the time you are ten years old, you have already been programmed in the way you will treat your future partner. The problem is, you forgot your programming, but your programs have not disappeared. Understanding your programming and your spouse's will give you great insight into finding where the love is.

- **Name your enemy.** We all have one. Most of us think of ourselves as good people, and we want good things, so why do we keep listening to that little dark voice inside our heads? Identifying, naming, and turning that invasive voice into a kind of "assistant" will be a key to making good relationship decisions.

- **Take 100 percent responsibility—clean the mess.** This might be a difficult idea at first, but most people appreciate that negativity attracts negativity. Here, I'll give you the tools to take responsibility for—and control of—all the negatives in your life, even the ones you didn't create, and transform them into positives.

- **Choose her.** Women need love and affection, but they also want to know what a guy stands for. By understanding her passion to be chosen and finding and following your purpose in life, you lay the groundwork for being admired—and for the relationship you really wanted all along.

- **Execute the mission—ride the wave.** How you're feeling can give you everything you want in a relationship and in life. People often talk about "being in the zone" or "riding the wave." Every single moment is an opportunity to be on the wave or to get bumped off it. I'll explain how shifting your awareness will allow you to ride the wave and bring good things into your life.

Throughout this book, you will find Target Packages with Reconnaissance and High-Resolution Intelligence. They will explain dynamics at work in our relationships and why so many problems we experience are not of our own making but are inherited. Target Packages will help you develop Actions-On Plans for saving your marriage. If they have access to High-Resolution Intelligence before a mission, smart SEALs use it. Once you have done the necessary preparation, you'll be ready to engage in Direct-Action Operations for the most important mission of your life: saving yourself and your marriage.

I'll share my own story along the way and the stories of other men I've helped as a friend and in my capacity as a life coach. The good news is that if we take 100 percent responsibility for these issues, even the ones we didn't create, things will change for the better. I'll explain how this process works. Execution Orders appear at the end of every chapter, giving you guidance on how to build and apply practical tools to heal your relationship.

The final chapters focus on the concrete lifestyle and mental choices that men can make to stop the negative momentum in their marriages and maintain the relationships they wanted from the beginning.

We all want to be happy. You hold in your hands a tool that will help you to achieve that happiness.

CHAPTER 1

FROM DISASTER TO AWAKENING

I am the problem with my marriage—and I can fix it.

I n 2003, after more than a dozen years as a Navy SEAL, I found myself in a fierce battle on a mountaintop in Afghanistan.

My daughter had been born the month before, on February 24, and the navy gave me leave for the birth. The day I returned from leave, I stepped off a CH-47 at the forward operating base and was welcomed by the guys. We had a little get-together to celebrate the birth. The next day, we were supposed to go shooting with some Afghan soldiers. We woke up early and spent the whole day firing rounds.

At the end of the day, we received intelligence that a checkpoint about an hour away was going to be overrun by Al-Qaeda that night. We immediately loaded up and started on the drive.

We arrived at Checkpoint 47, on the Pakistani border, as the sun was nearly setting. The light there can be weak and diffuse, but that evening, it was extremely clear. You could see all the way into an obscure city on the Pakistani side. In the distance, we saw vehicles drive up a dirt road, pull over, and unload heavy equipment. They clearly were preparing for an attack, but they were on the Pakistani side, so we couldn't engage; it would have been an international incident. We collected intelligence, identified where everyone was, and waited.

The tension before an anticipated attack is intense. I don't remember being scared, but there was so much adrenaline coursing through my body that my hand shook as I created the intel report in SALUTE format: the numbers of vehicles, the number of men, their exact locations, what weapons they had, the expected time of attack. The battle was expected to go down at midnight, and my state of preparedness was less than ideal. My head was cloudy from the trip home and the previous night's party. My marriage was a mess, my family life almost nonexistent, and I was not being a faithful, supportive husband or a good father. The bittersweet trip to see my new daughter had highlighted all the things I wanted and all the ways I was failing to achieve them. I was emotional, jetlagged, and sleep-deprived. My timeline was so screwed up, I didn't know who, what, or where I was.

And now we were getting ready to fight all night.

I took the first watch and let my buddy Mike sleep. When it was Mike's turn, I had dozed for maybe half an hour before 105-millimeter shells smashed into the mountains around us. A 105-millimeter shell is about as tall as a man's leg. I had body armor and a helmet on, but if that shell hits you, you're dead. It doesn't matter what you're wearing. It doesn't matter if you're in a tank.

Our position was getting hammered with these shells. A dozen to twenty exploded around us and the surrounding valley. Air support was called. They spotted enemy fighters on a Pakistan-side mountain range and then alerted us to a group one hundred yards north of our position. Suddenly, the whole mountain erupted in DShK fire—that's heavy Soviet artillery. We hammered the close targets with 40 "Mike-Mike" explosive golden eggs launched from a M-79 grenade launcher. Air support dropped several five-hundred-pound white phosphorous bombs on the far mountainside. "Willie Pete" bombs, as they're known, burn fiercely and create intense smoke. The entire mountainside glowed with fire as the bombs rained down, gunfire roaring all around us.

As I looked out, the mountain became a white inferno, and the chaos and violence outside seemed to echo the turmoil raging within me. I crested a hill to get a better situational awareness and saw a man crawling in a trench. As I was about to pull the trigger, he looked up and screamed that he was "Speedy," our interpreter. I was glad I'd paused to see if he was armed.

When we did the battle damage assessment the next day, a lot of the enemy had died, and all of us were okay. The border checkpoint was secure.

Still, it had been a close call. Certain situations make you step back and reassess your life, and on the drive back, I started thinking about what a bad husband I was. I had cheated on Samantha, my wife, again and again. We fought all the time. I wasn't there for her or for my kids. I didn't interact with them the way that a good husband and father should. I wasn't the man that I wanted to be.

After that battle, I pictured the funeral I might have had—the honor guard, flag-draped coffin, and speeches about bravery and sacrifice. *Taps* sounding as mourners wept. It was a funeral fit for a national hero, but my family would have a different view. At the funeral I imagined, my wife and kids would know everything I'd done. They would be full of hurt and sorrow because of my behavior. They would know what I was really like, and they would feel awful because I hadn't looked after them.

That gap, between the heroic image presented to the nation and the image my family would see—an image of the *real* me—made my heart sink.

Face-to-face with my mortality on that drive, I thought, *It doesn't have to be this way.* I remembered when I was thirteen years old and read the Ten Commandments. Back then, I had wondered, *Who wouldn't follow these rules? Why does this even have to be written down? Do not commit adultery? Of course not. Who would cheat on his wife?*

At thirteen, the way to behave honorably had seemed obvious. On that fateful day, I wasn't sure where I had gone wrong, but I thought, *I can change who I am. I will change who I am. I am going to be a good husband. I'm going to be a good father. I am going to be the man I want to be. And getting back to the Ten Commandments, those rules that had seemed so simple and true in boyhood would be the way to do it. Religion would put me on the right path.*

Sounds fantastic, right?

Well, it was, except I didn't know that the way that I was programmed to get back on the straight and narrow would be the straw that broke the camel's back (the camel, in this case, being my marriage). I was raised in a born-again Christian home, with people going to church and laying on hands and falling over. I had become a heathen, so obviously, I thought going back to church would fix everything.

When my deployment ended, I was stationed in Virginia. I started going to church regularly and became fascinated by Messianic Judaism, which combines Jewish traditions with a belief that Jesus, or *Yeshua Bin David* as they call Him, is the Messiah. I was struck by Messianic Jews' intense faith and beautiful rituals. This symbology, lost around 300 AD when Jewish rituals faded from the Christian Church, was incredible. It seemed a good fit for our family, too. My wife was Jewish. I was raised a born-again Christian. I decided that Messianic Judaism would be the middle ground where we could save our marriage.

I thought of this as a gift to my family, but I was also hell-bent on demanding their compliance. I didn't understand that, regardless of how beautiful I believed these things were, my family might not be receptive. Sam did not take well to my insistence that religion— my version of it—was the answer to our problems. She was Jewish but virtually agnostic, and the last thing she wanted was to have a Christian church rammed down her throat. I was judgmental of her and of everyone. Because I thought my newfound religion was *the* way to save our marriage and keep the family together, for me, everything came back to God and the Bible. I was like a reformed smoker trying to force people not to smoke—only I was a reformed cheater. There was only one way to do things, only one point of view. Anything Sam said or did that went against my interpretation of the Bible, she heard about.

And religion wasn't the only thing causing tension. As a SEAL, I was gone a lot for work, often for weeks or months at a time. When I returned home, I wanted immediately to be the man of the house. My first day back, I would insist, "No, I don't like this or that. We're doing it this other way." Whether it involved money or the kids or the house, it didn't matter. My insistence made Sam mad, and it made the kids question: *We did it this other way yesterday,* they would think. *What's this guy doing, barging in and changing our routine?*

There was immense stress in our house, and I blamed Sam. After all, I was the one doing all this work to save our marriage. I was the one going to church and trying to bring religion to my family. I was the one working hard as a SEAL and then trying to lead when I came home. I had stopped cheating and was being a loyal husband. I'd turned over a new leaf. Why wasn't she responding to all of my hard work?

Around this time, I deployed to Africa and met a pastor who was going to open up a farm in the Congo. The idea sounded great. I thought, *I'm going to help him.* It would provide food and jobs in an area that needed both desperately.

I actually sold my house in Virginia and gave most of the proceeds to this pastor so he could buy the land and other things he needed. Sam allowed me to do this because I said God was giving us a place to trust Him. Though skeptical, she also sort of wanted to see if something was really out there. She went along, but we didn't have a business plan for the farm or any real strategy. I thought I was putting all faith in God. I was expecting God to come through for my family and for money to come back.

I sent the money off—a sizeable amount—and we never saw a cent come back. The Holy-Roller train had left the station. Sam was stuck on it, with me driving, and she wasn't happy about the increasingly bumpy ride.

My religious antics had finally gone too far. She was done. But she still agreed to several more attempts of mine to save our marriage. I considered religious counselors, but religion was one of the reasons Sam was thinking of leaving me: no way was she going to see a Christian counselor. I went to the Command, and we arranged to talk to a psychologist. Because I was still very steeped in religion, however, I didn't have much faith in psychologists. Some of the things he said make sense now, but they didn't help me then.

RECONNAISSANCE

Eventually, I found Life Discoveries, Inc. and Larry Bilotta. I went through his course, and he and I started talking. Something about the program really resonated with me. I didn't get things right as a heathen, and I realized that I wasn't getting them right as a religious extremist. I needed help and a lot of it. That was the beginning of an intelligence-collection journey of trial and error that I have been on for almost a decade now. What I learned made sense for reestablishing happy, healthy relationships with my wife and kids. With many resources and a lot of deep reflection, I came to understand that women can actually be understood and that much of what Sam and I were going through wasn't really our fault. I discovered that the deck was stacked against us to the tune of guaranteed marriage failure from the very start. I'd had such bad intel for years that I was imagining enemies where none existed and chasing the wrong targets. I couldn't assemble a solid Target Package, much less engage in the Direct-Action Operations needed to save my marriage. That mission was doomed from the start.

I can't explain every detail of why my marriage was destined for failure, but Sam will concur that I couldn't make our kids or her feel completely safe and taken care of no matter what our family might endure. Many incidents undermined that feeling of security for Sam, but the core reason for my marriage falling apart was that I didn't know who I was or what I stood for.

Many times, I tried to show my wife that I loved her, but since I didn't know or love myself, I couldn't love anyone else. I went about it wrong because Sam had critical emotional needs unique to her that I couldn't comprehend or understand. (I'll discuss these in depth in the following chapters.)

I was upset because I realized a lot of damage had already been done. I finally was assembling a Target Package and beginning Direct-Action Operations by doing the things my wife needed, but I couldn't get traction. At last, I had a wonderful epiphany, which I regret greatly now. I decided that I would send the kids and her back to Australia, where Sam was born. This would make her happy, I thought, and indeed, she seemed quite happy about that plan.

I didn't have a plan to get to Australia myself, and as you might guess, none of this was well thought out. I simply told her that I had three years left in the navy. I'd get out early, and then we could be a family in Australia. She said she'd love that, so off she and the kids went to Australia. Within six months, she said to me, "You know what's great about this place? You're not here."

I realized too late why my marriage was failing and all the unwitting ways that I was responsible for its collapse. I felt like I was standing in the Rocky Mountains looking at a snow-covered peak about to become an avalanche. I could see the fissures in the snow. I thought, *I see the problems, and I see the solutions. I can fix this.* But I couldn't. It was too late for Sam and me. The marriage was essentially over long before I identified the problems, but of course, I was over-confident. I didn't believe it.

In Australia, Sam began dating someone from her past. I wasn't happy, but I thought, *Okay, stay calm, this is no problem.* Her new love interest was married, with two kids. He and his wife were going through a divorce, and Sam wanted to move in with him. I said, go ahead, move in with him. I knew this would be stressful for her. I'd worked hard for a year and a half to show her that I loved her. The stress of living with him and his children would take its toll, and when it did, I would be a pillar that she would be glad she still had.

The scenario started out much as I had imagined it. Sam got stressed about her new boyfriend's kids and his ex-wife. There are a lot of tensions built into that dynamic. In November 2009, we were on the phone. We'd been talking a lot in the previous months. I loved hearing her voice and hearing her sound supportive as she encouraged the kids to talk to me. As she walked around the boyfriend's house, I could tell that she was making sure he wasn't within earshot. She was contemplating leaving him to put our family back together. I was ecstatic because I could feel things falling into place for our family.

During one particular phone call, she said that she'd asked our son what he would think if they moved back in with Dad. I cried inside because I was so happy that the nightmare was finally ending.

I don't know exactly what happened next, but I do know the basis of life is freedom. All the years that I'd been a controlling ass were still fresh in Sam's mind. That great phone call happened, and then when we talked the next day, her voice had an edge. She told me she'd been thinking about what she'd said, and she wanted to rescind.

I felt a bomb drop on my head. I was devastated, but instead of being okay with her taking back the dream—the right response— I got upset. If I would have stayed cool, calm, and collected, who knows what could have happened. I should have realized that she felt like she would be coming back into a life where she would be controlled—a life she hated—again.

I did not fully grasp then that freedom truly is the basis of life. Given all we'd been through, all that she'd endured with me, it was a natural human response for her to fear being controlled again. It's human nature to prefer being free to feeling miserable in a situation where you have to act like you're happy.

Nothing was written in stone at this point. Sam needed somebody to talk to who could be loving, warm, and totally understanding of her woes at that moment in time. But she slammed the door shut, recalling my controlling nature toward her in the past. I just wanted my family back. I did not want to control her anymore. I did not want any of the things that she was terrified about. But despite these things, I wasn't the emotional rock that I needed to be when she was waffling on what she wanted.

HIGH-RESOLUTION INTELLIGENCE

There are seven phases to a woman returning to her mate, according to Life Discoveries, Inc. Over the years, as I've learned about what makes relationships work, I have helped a number of men turn their marriages around through understanding these seven phases. (We'll discuss them in detail in chapter 6.) The last phase is, "Why would I ever leave this guy?", but arriving at that last phase means getting on the right frequency, which requires a fair amount of focused work. Other phases involve her being flirtatious, giving various gestures, and indicating that she's interested. The phases cannot be rushed, and this book offers a guide to navigating your partner's return, giving her the responses she needs at the right times, and maintaining a supreme level of patience through the delicate process that could determine the rest of your life.

The last item in that list—patience—is perhaps the most important for men, who often want immediate results and gratification. "I don't want to go through the steps that will make things better in the long run, I just want success now." This is a typical male response. I know because it became my response with Sam. I had sent my kids to Australia, and I wanted them back. I wanted to raise them in a home where they felt safe and knew they were secure and happy.

When I responded to Sam, she wasn't at the final phase of return, the step in which a woman thinks, *Why would I ever leave this guy?* She might have been close to that phase. She was talking to me on a regular basis, and I understood the stress that she was under, and things between us had been progressing nicely.

So what went wrong after that fateful phone call? I reached too hard. It's that simple.

Here's an analogy: If you are skydiving and want to join a crew of three people who are in a connected formation, what do you do when you get close to them? Most people say, "Reach out and link arms." Seems obvious, right? Wrong. If you reach out your arms in skydiving, the relative wind pushes you away from where you want to go. Reaching for what you want is what any normal person would do, but in fact, by reaching out, you push yourself away from the target. In "free fall," you need to pull your arms back.

After that phone call when Sam rescinded her offer, I reached out, grabbing for what I wanted. I got extremely emotional. I was upset about her change of mind, and I let her know it in no uncertain terms. I felt like the world had been turned upside down. I was crushed. But my reaction gave her flashbacks to the way she'd been controlled when we were together. It was never my intention to be controlling again. I just wanted to be with my family because of the vow that I'd made to myself in 2003 to be a good husband and a good father.

But how was Sam to know or, really, believe this? She was thinking, *Darek might have been great for a year and a half, right before*

I moved to Australia, but he never showed me he cared about what was important to me and wasn't a good spouse for years before that. Now, she was in a stressful situation with another man, who was dissolving his family in Australia, and she remembered all the terrible things I had done. I reminded her again of all she hated, and she was forced to make a choice.

The trick to joining that circle in skydiving is to actually kick your legs out and to pull your arms in. Then you gently fingertip-grab the other person while your arms are tucked in like tiny Tyrannosaurus rex limbs. It's a restrained operation. You get closer by holding back.

I've shared this analogy to a number of men facing relationship trouble, and their partners came back because the men did not make a grab at the first sign of closeness. When their partners said,

> You get closer by holding back.

"I'm thinking about coming home for Christmas," the men replied, "That would be fun"—a response that was positive but also restrained. They did not demand. They did not send the signal saying, "Hey, you have to come home!"

If I could go back and provide High-Resolution Intelligence to the "me" who was frantic after the conversation when Sam backed out, I would say, *Look, buddy, you got punched in the nose, okay, but you're fine. Just go back to everything that you were doing before that setback, the things that made her call you in the first place. After you've calmed down, call her. Email her, explain what happened, and let her know she can do whatever she needs to feel free.*

I should have told Sam that I understood her recoiling at my emotional response, that I was staying where I was, and that for now, she should, too. I should have said that I appreciated what she said about our son wanting to come home, and that if she had further thoughts on that later, great. If not, that would be okay, too. I should have said that the main thing was how much I liked hearing her talk about the kids and just hearing her talk. Period. Words to that effect would have taken the pressure off of her.

Instead, I ignored the intel and focused on exactly what I didn't want. I lost all hope. I fell off the mountaintop, all the way to the bottom of the valley. I wish at the time I'd had the kind of intel I'll discuss in chapter 5, "Clean the Mess," which emphasizes focusing on what you want. Instead, like so many men in troubled relationships, I drifted away from the Mission Execution.

Sam's and my marriage was essentially over, though we didn't officially get divorced until 2010. I was despondent and in deep grief.

I was in San Diego at the time and decided to return to the Naval Special Warfare Development Group, but I was just going through the motions. If you've been a SEAL for a long time, you can get away with going through the motions for a while, but you also have men counting on you to make sure they stay alive. I screwed up a lot of little things. I remember, for instance, a night jump out of an airplane when the drop zone was right in front of us. A piece of my equipment wasn't working, but instead of just flying with the group and not worrying about it, I kept playing with the problem gear and landed around five kilometers off target. That's dangerous. I put myself in considerable danger and the other guys, too. If it had happened on a combat jump in-theater, they would have had to come get me.

In the same manner, I decided to get into another relationship when it looked like my marriage was finally done. I wanted Sam to think, *That girl thinks he's valuable. Maybe I made a mistake.* This technique can be effective, but it has consequences that affect unseen parts of your relationship. Besides that, you look like a manipulative ass. Eventually, though, I realized that the divorce was real and that I needed a substantial relationship. I started dating a second woman, and it was much better, but there was still a lot of stray "emotional voltage" within me. You just don't come out of my kind of situation without having long-lasting glitches in the system.

Today, after a life-changing awakening, followed by many years of reading, studying, and reflecting about love and relationships, the hard work has paid off. This book is being written after climbing back up the mountain, the result of an arduous learning process that I required to find life again, to rediscover a reason to live. My goal here is to make that process less difficult for other men whose relationships are lacking, on the ropes, and in danger of failing.

DIRECT-ACTION OPERATIONS

There are many tools that will resonate with you as you read this book, but if you learn only the ability to *take 100 percent responsibility* for your life and to have complete acceptance of and appreciation for every aspect of your experience, then you will go a long way toward making your life more tolerable, and even incredibly enjoyable, for you and those you love.

One key piece of intel you will need to take Direct-Action Operations has already been touched on. It involves a revised version of the Golden Rule. Treat your mate not as *you* want to be treated, but as *she* wants to be treated. Being able to understand and apply this one concept in my marriage with Sam would have made a world of difference, and so, I will explore it in detail in the next chapter, alongside the key ideas about how men and women are motivated and how their emotional needs differ.

EXECUTION ORDERS

Identify your wife's background and identify your background, and key in on logical reasons why arguments are happening, not because anything is wrong with either of you but simply because you were raised in different homes. See your wife's behavior as logical from a viewpoint of how she was raised instead of being angry at her for not doing something how you want it done because that is how you were raised; this will allow you both some much needed grace and peace right now.

CHAPTER 2

THE REAL GOLDEN RULE

Treat others as they *wish to be treated.*

Men and women have very different needs that the opposite sex doesn't understand or care about. Partners in a relationship are in tune with their own needs but rarely appreciate those of their spouses. Ignorance of these needs and how they vary according to gender is a root cause chipping away at a marriage. Seeing and meeting your partner's needs is a vital step in getting your marriage where you want it to be. It's something that husbands can begin doing immediately, on their own, to change the tone of their relationships, getting it out of trouble or keeping it healthy before unhappiness appears.

HIGH-RESOLUTION INTELLIGENCE

We are going to focus on women for the moment. Above all else, a woman wants to be chosen, and her debut "chosen event" is her wedding day. We will explore this further in chapter 6. This process of *choosing her* falls into two distinct categories, since a woman who feels emotionally and financially secure is a very happy girl. Women come from different backgrounds, so how these specific needs translate varies from woman to woman, but all women have these two core needs: emotional and financial security. Making it possible for the woman in your life to feel chosen, as well as emotionally and financially secure, is key to your having that happy marriage you signed up for. Usually, when a woman is upset with someone in her life, whatever she might say outwardly, deep down she is saying, *Hey, you are upsetting my emotional-security needs*, or *You're wrecking my financial-security needs. And I'm really, really unhappy!*

> Seeing and meeting your partner's needs is a vital step in getting your marriage where you want it to be.

When women get together, they won't use the exact words "emotional and financial security," but whatever issues they discuss usually add up to one or both of these two core needs. Even highly independent women, who don't need a man's emotional or financial security, prefer that you're supportive of their independent quality.

Supporting independence can be another way to meet a woman's emotional security needs.

Men often don't understand or care about women's needs, because they are so focused on their own. They have a vague sense that their wives' or girlfriends' surface needs reflect something deeper, but that "something" is rarely ever communicated. It's as if their wives are speaking Japanese, while the men speak German. Men hear the words, but they can't seem to understand what their wives are really saying.

Often, one of the reasons that a man can't understand the woman in his life is that his two greatest needs are dramatically different from hers. Men's two core needs are for sexual intimacy and respect—needs vastly different from a woman's two core needs of emotional security and financial security.

Let's look at an example:

> Joe and Sally are married, and when the kids don't clean up their rooms, Joe yells at them. Sally's reaction is usually: "Joe, when you yell at the kids, it really bothers me." The way Joe interprets Sally's words is that he and she are no longer "on the same page." Joe wants his wife to agree with his way of doing things, so when she doesn't, he feels disrespected.
>
> For Sally, whose top priority is emotional security, it is vital that the kids feel safe around their parents. This is what she is trying to convey, but Joe's reaction is, "You're not backing me up as my wife." Sally's emotional security has been upset by Joe's yelling at the kids, yet Joe doesn't appreciate any of this from Sally's point of view. Joe is not meeting Sally's need for emotional security—and he's not even aware of it. From Sally's perspective, Joe has com-

pletely missed the real issue, and from Joe's perspective, Sally has completely missed the real issue. It's as if they are speaking foreign languages to each other. Sally says, "Joe, don't yell at the kids." Joe says, "Sally, you need to back me up." But what Sally means is, "Joe, support my emotional need to feel secure by making the kids comfortable and speaking calmly to them." Joe really means, "Sally, respect me by recognizing that I need order in this house, and dirty rooms disrespect me."

But communicating what they actually mean would require understanding each other's true emotional needs.

This is a typical recipe for conflict. Sally gets tied in knots because she wants to change Joe's behavior, even as she fears Joe's reaction. Because of her fear, she brings up the problem awkwardly and defensively. Joe sees her defensiveness as an attempt to control his behavior and as disrespect. Joe is completely ignoring Sally's core need for emotional security. All communication breaks down, causing distance and conflict.

How Joe and Sally navigate the situation—and the degree to which they can start to verbalize and recognize each other's core needs—determines how explosive it will become. Rather than sounding critical, Sally could pull Joe aside and be affectionate and loving, making gestures that show respect and intimacy, and then say, "Hey, can we come up with a different way to get the kids to clean up their rooms? I don't think yelling at them is working." With this approach, Joe would be far more likely to be receptive to a different solution.

Rather than focusing on Sally's concern as a threat to his authority, Joe could listen attentively to her problem while showing her affection—a sign that he is in tune with her emotional security. Think of this as vital intelligence-gathering that can help husbands prepare for the mission to save their marriages. When he attempts to understand Sally's needs and concerns, Joe is gathering High-Resolution Intelligence on his wife, insight that is vital to Mission Success. Each spouse could address the issue in a way that fulfills and recognizes the other's core needs and thus avoid conflict. They can, in short, learn to speak each other's languages. Too often, however, this doesn't happen, even though both partners want what's best for the kids and each other.

I faced endless scenarios just like this in my marriage—most couples do. I did not understand my wife's need for emotional and financial security at all. It meant nothing to me. I had grown up, like many readers, being taught that we should live by the Golden Rule: do unto others as you would have them do unto you. The problem with applying this rule to marriage is that it leaves out other people's personalities and the needs of the opposite sex. If you live by this rule literally, then you're looking at everything through the lens of what *you* want in life and how *you* want to be treated—not how your partner wants to be treated.

In my marriage to Sam, if I felt I wasn't getting the respect or intimacy I craved, and thus wasn't getting my core needs met, my solution was to yell, to get upset about not being supported as the man of the family. I was a bull in a china shop all the time. German was my language, and I had no interest in learning Japanese—I didn't even know this other language existed.

Like Joe and Sally—and most couples—Sam and I experienced tension over how we dealt with our children. If my son didn't do something Sam asked him to, I would come home and insist, "Hey, you've got to listen to your Mum." I would give him a chance and then say, "Okay, you're not listening to Mum? You're going to do some push-ups." That did not go over well with Sam, because it was militant and punitive. She did not want this threat of push-ups hanging over his head all the time. It was not something that had ever happened in her house growing up, and rather than discuss this punishment with her in advance, I just went ahead and dished it out.

We were speaking different languages, but amplifying the tension and miscommunication was the fact that we also had different natures. I have a hard nature. I'm a Navy SEAL, and as I'm sure is the case in many offices and on construction sites, at my job I faced a lot of urgent tasks that needed to get done. I worked with a crew of men who were all speaking the language of respect to each other on a consistent basis because they shared this core need. We respected each other's opinions because we had a goal in mind and were marching toward it at about a hundred miles an hour on fire. We paused only if necessary and only if it made tactical sense. The thing that we were going after was going to be accomplished—no question about it.

People who are hard natured are success oriented. The thing that makes them feel best in life is when they achieve a goal. Sam, like many women—certainly not all—is soft natured. A soft-natured person relates success in life to cultivating great relationships. By making my son do push-ups, I was demanding that he show respect to Sam and me, but this was not her priority at all. She wanted to build trust and a positive relationship with our son. I had zero intel on her needs and attitudes, however, so I didn't understand this. Both of us had good intentions—there just wasn't a lot of overlap in our communication styles. Neither of us was learning the other's language, and neither of us wanted to. It's impossible to gather the High-Resolution Intelligence needed to save a marriage if you can't even say *hello* in your wife's language.

This communication gulf plays out in all sorts of ways in relationships. One of the most noticeable is in the realm of affection, sex, and intimacy. I was not doing the things that were important to Sam, and I wasn't getting my relationship right with the kids. At the same time, I was a healthy male, and sexual intimacy was one of my core needs. Studies suggest that a man feels a powerful urge to be intimate every two or three days. But if he's not providing the right "environment" for his wife to feel loved (man translation: foreplay), from her perspective, it's not going to happen. Before anyone gets too excited, let me explain that the foreplay I'm talking about is the kind that provides emotional security. This includes the mundane but vital work of understanding your partner and accepting and adopting her ways of enjoying a great life, along with cleaning the house, shopping, picking the kids up from school, helping with their homework, preparing a meal, and just plain listening.

Most women work incredibly hard, taking care of hearth and home and the children. They go to work, try to look their best, and take care of the million things on their plates every day. The more burdens a partner can take from her shoulders, the more she will appreciate him, and on a practical level, the more time she has to offer sexual intimacy. On an emotional level, the more that he addresses her other needs, the more willing she will be to have sex with him. In my relationship with Sam, two or three days would go by, and I would start giving the hints: *Okay, it's time.* For me, this wasn't just a sexual desire but also a way to show Sam that I loved her. From her perspective, I was not showing her that I loved her in any of the ways important to her, so why would she want sexual intimacy with me?

As my frustration grew, I would try guilt trips, manipulation, anything I could to get her in bed. It was exhausting for Sam. She was not getting any help, and I turned into just another child she had to manage. Only I wasn't some innocent eight-year-old. This kid was her adult husband, a big idiot who was dying to get her into bed but didn't know how to be a man, husband, or father.

This became our weekly routine: me trying to have sex and her acquiescing now and then. Sometimes she agreed in more exciting ways than others, and sometimes her attitude only conveyed, *Okay, hurry up, get it over with*. I didn't deserve affection, so sex became something she saw as her "wifely duty."

Women want to be romanced. They want to enjoy their lives, to feel easy and free. They don't want to submit to sex simply because "he needs this right now." They will say yes sometimes, here and there, perhaps many times, but men, you are taking money out of the bank account every time that happens. If you don't replenish it with the kind of emotional support I've described, then the account will go broke. Sam was an absolutely amazing wife, and if I'd pulled even a thousandth of my weight at home, I wouldn't be writing this book.

You need to treat your partner as *she* wants to be treated, not as you want to be treated. Respect her language. If you go to Japan and you don't take off your shoes at the door and demonstrate respect, people might smile and pretend everything is fine—that culture values politeness—but you will not be truly welcome there. If you do take off your shoes and follow the local customs and respect the culture, then things will go well.

I have discussed the way that men's core needs (respect and intimacy) and women's core needs (emotional and financial security) can be met using the real Golden Rule (treat others as *they* wish to be treated) in order to build a healthy relationship. I also have discussed how respecting the differing values of hard and soft natures can strengthen trust and understanding. But to put the real Golden Rule completely into practice, we must also consider personalities.

RECONNAISSANCE

Identify your wife and yourself in the following personality profiles.

THE FOUR PERSONALITY TYPES

Psychologists assess personalities in various ways, but experts have identified four main personality types, going back to the Greek physician Hippocrates, around 400 BC. Hippocrates associated these personality types with "bodily humors" and labeled them as "sanguine, choleric, melancholic, and phlegmatic."

In the last forty years, many authors have written about the same four types of personality, a classic example being the book titled *Your Personality Tree* by Florence Littauer.

Expanding on the ideas we have from Hippocrates and books such as *Your Personality Tree*, we can say that people's personalities fit into four main categories: **Joyful** (Sanguine), **Easygoing** (Phlegmatic), **Precise** (Melancholic), and **Command** (Choleric). Each personality type carries its own **value system**, which its bearers live by. If you don't understand a person's particular value system, trouble soon follows.

For instance, I now realize that Sam was an Easygoing person, and the most important things for Easygoing people are respect (for themselves and others) and getting along with everyone. Everyone must keep peace and act in harmony, or visitors are not welcome. Because I didn't know this when we were together, I mistakenly insisted that my Easygoing wife tolerate my ways as a Joyful person, displaying the less-desirable traits of that personality. I believed that people were wrong for any number of reasons and would, therefore, justify some kind of action or judgment against them.

Joyful people (like me) love to have a good time. As the name implies, they value fun, and for them, anything goes. They become frustrated when somebody criticizes them or when mundane details prevent them from doing what they find interesting and exciting. At their best, they are enthusiastic, optimistic, inspirational, funny, loving, and sincere. But at their worst, they talk too much, exaggerate, seem phony, forget responsibilities, lack discipline, and are easily distracted.

Easygoing people want everyone to get along, so conflict is hard on them. At their best, they are confident, consistent, witty, patient, peaceful, and very good listeners. But at their worst, they are fearful and worried, indecisive, shy, unmotivated, resentful of being pushed, and resistant to change.

The most important thing for **Precise people** is for others to be sensitive to their feelings. They want everything perfect, and this is not easily accomplished, so they work hard in their attempts to get everything right. At their best, they are faithful, persistent, idealistic, creative, organized, and thoughtful. But at their worst, they constantly think of negatives. They are moody and depressed, feel guilty, spend too much time planning, and set their standards too high.

The most important thing for **Command people** is to be appreciated for what they do and to get things done. They don't worry about other people's feelings. As you can imagine, this creates more than a little resentment. The key to understanding a Command person is knowing that, more than anything, they want to be appreciated for what they do. They can bear an incredible amount of weight while getting a lot of things done. At their best they are great leaders, confident, goal oriented, independent, quick, and quite bold. But at their worst they can become bossy, impatient, temperamental, demanding, and arrogant.

As you can see, each value system has its own quirks, and underneath these quirks are real people. The more High-Resolution Intelligence you have on your wife—her quirks and personality type—the more readily you can arrive at a give-and-take relationship that works. It is vital that you know which of these four personality types fits your partner.

ACTIONS-ON PLAN

What do I mean by a give-and-take relationship? Let's say that you are a Precise person and that it is important to you to have people follow through and do what they say they will do. Being on time is highly prized by your particular value system. You have experienced many people in your life who were not on time or didn't do what they said they were going to do. When you meet someone who always does what they say they're going to do and is always on time—or if late, calls to let you know in advance—there is a mutual respect in your relationship because this is a person who appreciates your value system. And you respect their values. This is healthy give-and-take.

If somebody is doing things you like, and they are avoiding the things you don't like, then they are welcome in your value system. You appreciate them, and it's human nature to have a give-and-take relationship. Reciprocally, that's when you will want to do things they value whenever possible, even though they might be from a different value system. This is key to "the awakening" that I discussed in chapter 1.

This is an amazing moment in your relationship. You are doing what your wife appreciates and needs, and it's possible that nobody in her life has ever done these things for her. It's as if she's getting a heart-felt gift for the first time in her life, and she loves it! It's as if you are finally speaking her native language of Japanese and making the effort to understand that language. You actually understand, for example, her need for emotional and financial security. You're going to Japan and taking off your shoes. You're being respectful, and you understand the nuances of the culture.

Because you have respected the customs and values of her particular personality type, she gives you the gift of the samurai sword. This "samurai sword" might be nothing you actually care about because you are from a different value system, but that samurai sword might be her highest honor, such as a spotless house. A spotless house might be nothing that you discuss with other men, but it's your wife's gift to you because she is trying to participate in a give-and-take relationship. She is doing her best to get it right, based on her own understanding and what *she* appreciates most. Seek to first understand your wife's value system, and make the effort to learn and respect her customs, and then she will give you that samurai sword, which is her love, her acceptance, and her attraction to you. What do you do with that gift then? You must be careful to never lose it. You can easily overlook that she is giving you her highest reward and end up ignoring or irritating her because her treasured gift isn't your idea of a treasured gift. But you would be shooting yourself in the foot if you were to undervalue that heart-felt gift.

Respecting and understanding your wife is an important first step. Ask yourself if you have been respecting your wife's value system. I'm talking about the whole package: emotional and financial security, as well as what she needs because she has a personality that is Joyful, Precise, Command, or Easygoing. Have you been speaking her language? Have you made the effort to collect enough intel to determine her foundational value system? Have you been treating your wife the way she wants to be treated, or have you been treating her the way *you* want to be treated?

When I take stock of my own marriage, I can honestly say that after finally understanding the things that were most important to Sam, I can count the number of times I genuinely showed her that I loved her. I felt great love for her, but it didn't show, not to her. She is Easygoing and has a very different set of values than I do. When I thought I was showing her that I loved her, I was actually trying to turn her into me, a Joyful guy.

Collecting High-Resolution Intelligence on your wife's value system doesn't do much good if you don't start making the gestures that are meaningful to her personality's value system. Learning about a person's value system and focusing on it is not easy. With Sam, I should have understood her need for everyone to get along. I should have developed a Target Package that included easing her burdens and giving her more personal time. My Direct-Action Operations should have included doing the laundry, cleaning the house, and spending more time caring for the children. Instilling a live-and-let-live attitude. A lot of these things would have conveyed that my love for her was real because I understood her Easygoing value system.

But all the tasks that would have made her life easier were boring to me, just as they are for a lot of men. However, the payoff is worth it. Remember, no matter how much you dislike the work you must do, it is essentially romance: foreplay from the female perspective. Not sexual foreplay but foreplay of a deeper, more important variety. It is far more powerful and a much bigger turn-on for the girl who has your heart.

There are ways to accept the work you must do and even make it enjoyable. As you fold the laundry, imagine you are tracing your finger along her panty line. As you get up early to make breakfast for the family, think of this gesture as brushing her hair aside to deliver a kiss on her neck. As a man, you can imagine this work as literal, sexual foreplay because it will have the same effect for you. Patience is the key to this process. You did not grow distant overnight, and closeness might not happen in a day or a week. But persistence pays off, and even if your wife has already moved out, the improvement in your relationship will not be in a straight line. In the short term, depending on how distant you have become, your wife might actually seem annoyed by your positive gestures and your attempts to care for her unique value system. This is normal, and it's important for you to stay the course. If you keep the switch flipped to positive, maintaining your positive mentality in everything you do for her, then magic *will* happen in your relationship.

> If you keep the switch flipped to positive, maintaining your positive mentality in everything you do for her, then magic will happen in your relationship.

RECONNAISSANCE

Dave, a man I counseled as his marriage hit the rocks, is a good example. Dave and I worked together doing security in Africa. He was coordinating things from Africa, and I was planning from Germany. Dave is about my age, athletic, a husband and father. When we finally met in person, for some reason we started talking about marriage.

Dave wrote about the time he and I spent together. Here is his account:

> Certain things in life happen for a reason. The operation that Darek (Chief Laviolette) and I were on was one of those occasions. I met Darek on the airport tarmac in a

faraway place. It was a quick nod and handshake as we tossed gear from one plane to another. There was some small talk, but we were mostly focused on getting there and on the assignment. On location, we stored our gear, conducted some briefings, and discussed the OP plan, gaming it to discuss possible contingencies for the assignment. Perhaps Darek and I hit it off because we were clearly older than the rest of his team. When we were satisfied, we knocked off for the night. Darek and I stayed and talked and became a little better acquainted. I told him about my wife and daughter, and I'm sure he could tell that I was excited about how much my daughter loved swimming and gymnastics. For whatever reason, I also ended up talking to Darek about how severely strained my relationship was with my wife. I explained how travel, operations, and assignments over the years had gotten to both my wife and daughter and that things were at a tipping point. I was angry and confused. I didn't think my wife got it. My job was important, and it was providing a great life for her. I was angry because I felt she was no longer showing the support she once had. I was confused because I was listless; I was the type of guy who could fix a problem, and now I had a problem I couldn't fix. I was sad because I still loved my wife, and of course, I loved my daughter. The thought of losing them was a hard pill to swallow.

With the first phase of our operation over, we loaded up for our onward. Phase II was in another location, and it would take time to get there. I have spoken to Darek many times over the years about how this flight SEALED my marriage. We loaded up a C-130 transport; it is a loud propeller-driven workhorse originally manufactured in the fifties, and it is still in wide use today. It is much smaller than its C-5 and C-17 cousins, so seating is at a premium. Our gear was in the middle, and we found space along the fuselage to settle in for the ride. I was sitting next to Darek on some cargo netting. Shortly after takeoff, I noticed how young Darek's guys looked. He told me it was their first rodeo, that most were not married, and those who were married were newlyweds, relatively speaking. I remembered being like those guys—young, idealistic, ready to take on the world. My ideals haven't changed, but over the years, my eyes have been opened to how a job can wear on you and how it can affect a marriage.

For whatever reason, Darek decided to share a bit of his life with me over the roar of the Hercules engines while sitting on that cargo net. Darek told me he had not seen his children in two years. He told me about his wife, about the ups and downs of his marriage, and that after it collapsed, how she returned to Australia, kids in tow. He told me how things had become so bad that they had resorted to "snail mail," and what little communication he now had was done in letters. He sent them, but none returned. I was silent. The silence was so protracted that Darek thought it wise to break the ice. He said to me, "I better start laughing now, or we will both end up crying." I appreciated him lightening the atmosphere, but I just sat there staring at him almost in disbelief. I was trying to imagine his pain, and I wondered if the same marriage implosion was in store for me.

Darek told me a story that he got from a Dr. Glenn Pfau leadership course he had attended. I've passed it along to many people.

While the audience was seated in an auditorium, Dr. Pfau walked onto the stage juggling two glass spheres and a rubber ball. He talked about the importance of work versus family. While juggling, he began to bounce a rubber ball up and down with one hand, the glass spheres still rotating in the air with the other. He said the rubber ball represented work. The harder bounces symbolized the effort people put into their jobs. The harder we worked, the more reward we seemed to get, so the ball bounced higher. He began to bounce the ball lightly. This symbolized putting in less effort, ergo less reward, worse results, and a much lower bounce of the ball. He then let the ball drop. This symbolized retirement or termination. Dr. Pfau said that work, like the rubber ball, was something you could always pick up again and begin to bounce, which he demonstrated. He then looked into the audience and said the glass spheres were symbolic of family, and if not constantly maintained and cared for, which he demonstrated by keeping them aloft, they would come crashing down. At that moment, a loud crash resonated throughout the auditorium. Dr. Pfau had dropped the glass spheres, and all that remained were broken shards of glass. Dr. Pfau, still in front of the crowd tossing the rubber ball up and down, looked at the shards. Once dropped or neglected, the family will break, never to be put back together the same way again.

Darek's story had a big effect on me. After phase II of our operation ended without incident, I exchanged contact details with Darek and his guys, and we said our good-byes. Sometimes that's all you're left with.

This time was different. I ran into Darek and his guys a few more times, as they were in my AOR (area of responsibility), which provided some opportunity for dinner and beers. The conversation would inevitably turn to family, kids, and marriage. I stayed in touch with Darek and his guys when they rotated back stateside. My contact with Darek's guys kept a conduit open that allowed us to stay in touch.

A year later, I made a trip to Virginia Beach while my wife and daughter visited family elsewhere. I called Darek. We chatted, and he asked me how things really were between my wife and me. I told him we had been in counseling for a year and things were tenuous. The counseling was hard because I was constantly being sent on assignment, so the consistency needed to make progress was significantly lacking. I was in a difficult spot. I was returning overseas, and I was unsure if my wife and daughter would be coming with me. I loved my wife and couldn't imagine life without her. My daughter was the lightning in the bottle. She was everything to me. I knew a father's role is ever important and that if my marriage failed, if they didn't return with me, my relationship would be broken, never to be the same—like all those glass shards in the auditorium. The conversation was fairly one-sided. Darek listened, and I talked things through. Darek offered guidance he thought would serve me best to make the right decision for my marriage. I told him that I had reflected on many things over the past year, and that I had come to the conclusion that my wife didn't cause my anger, confusion, or sadness at all. My own selfishness was the root of our problems. It is instinct in the human animal to defend itself when it is injured. I believe my myopic view over the years about caring about my job, work, operations, safety, and my guys' safety made me defensive and prevented me from meeting the needs of my daughter, my wife, and my marriage.

I called Darek from the airport before heading back overseas. I told him my wife and daughter were with me and that I knew there was work to do but that I wasn't afraid to put in the time I needed to save my marriage and repair damage. After almost two decades of taking care of what the United States government needed, I realized that, while important, it was a rubber ball that could be bounced lightly and picked back up if dropped. I wanted to give my attention to the glass balls—the things that were more important to me.

Postscript: It has been five years, and I'm on another assignment, but my marriage is SEALED. My wife and I are truly happy. It took time, and there were many tears in the process. However, my wife and daughter know they are first for me in all ways. I am a better communicator and listener and became a better father and husband.

I maintain that the talk with Darek on that C-130 was a life-changing event for me. My daughter was recently accepted into the college of her dreams. She leaves home knowing that I made the choice to fight instead of give up. She leaves knowing how much I love her and her mother, that their well-being became my focus. She leaves knowing the glass ball won't ever fall.

Dave's wife sent me an email later, thanking me profusely for talking some sense into him and painting a realistic picture of what divorce would mean. A few years later, his daughter had a girlfriend whose parents were getting divorced. That girl was only able to see her father every so often, and Dave's daughter said to him, "Aren't you happy that you decided to stay with Mommy? That way you can see me every day!"

That story left me in tears, happy that Sam's lessons in my life had saved Dave's family.

EXECUTION ORDERS

You and your wife almost definitely look at the world through a different lens. Gain an understanding of what she wants in her life regarding emotional and financial security. Spend some time thinking about how people from your personality type want to experience life. Spend more time considering your wife's personality, and believe that she has a different way to experience "happily ever after." By understanding her personality and incorporating things valued by her personality, your actions will be well received, even if she doesn't act like it at first.

Once you understand their personality and needs, you will want to do things they value whenever possible, even though they might be from a different value system. This is key to "the awakening" that I discussed in chapter 1.

CHAPTER 3

PATTERNS
OF LIFE

Our "program" for marriage is formed by age ten.

HIGH-RESOLUTION
INTELLIGENCE

When I was stationed in Virginia Beach, Sam and I had a friend from San Diego whose sister came to visit. Our friend decided to have a little get-together during the visit. Nothing fancy, just a few drinks and a barbecue in their backyard. It didn't matter much what time we arrived or what we wore. This should have been a relaxing evening to look forward to, but I was never relaxed in those days.

Getting ready for an event was always a tense time for Sam and me. On this night, she was doing her best to get dressed and get the kids ready and, the whole time, I was trying to rush her out the door. While she was getting the kids prepared and putting on makeup and taking care of whatever needed to be done, we had this constant banter going on that accomplished nothing but stressing her out. Before the evening even started, I was unwittingly turning something fun into a chore.

Finally, the kids were ready and Sam was dressed. She wore a blue skirt with a cute top, simple but classy; she always looked classy, not that I took the time to compliment her or even notice. I was too concerned with keeping everything on track and getting everyone into the car. The kids were neat and well behaved, as always. This, too, was Sam's doing. I hadn't helped any in that department or shown my appreciation for the great job she did with them.

We arrived at our friend's house, where several of us who always hung out were gathered, and sat on the deck in the backyard. It was a beautiful summer night in Virginia Beach: friends gathered, drinks poured, and a delicious aroma wafted from the smoker—one of those Big Green Eggs.

During dinner, our friend's sister became tipsy and was obviously drunk by the end of it. This was after I'd had my awakening and was convinced that religion was *the* way to save my marriage. I related earlier how I had thrust my newfound beliefs—heavily influenced by my upbringing as a born-again Christian—onto Sam, but it didn't stop there. All night, I kept circling the conversation back to religion. I don't remember exactly what religious topics I talked about on this particular night, but there was always something godly for me to expound on.

When you're around somebody like the person I was then, it is common to find yourself stuck in a sermon, feeling suffocated or wishing you could escape. For anyone who endured this part of my life—I'm greatly embarrassed, and I apologize.

As I've said, Sam is Jewish and pretty much agnostic, so imagine what it was like for her to be sitting with this Holy-Roller—the vocal, reformed, born-again Christian that I had become. At every opportunity, I held forth on the one topic guaranteed to make her want to crawl under a rug and die. I was constantly beating people over the head with a Bible. I might have sounded nice and genuine, but, in fact, I was judging the hell out of everyone. On the night in question, I focused on intoxication, but at other times I lectured people who were pro-choice or who were behaving in any of the many ways that I judged immoral.

This was typical behavior for me then, but on this particular night, I had the added outrage of the drunk party guest around our kids to fuel my fire. Oh yes, in my eyes, her behavior was a complete outrage, an abomination, something so egregious that I personally had to deal with it. A party guest got drunk—at someone else's party—and I reacted as if she'd murdered someone in front of us on the lawn.

Before long, the drunk woman went upstairs and passed out on the bed, and I felt that I was not only justified in going to talk to her about God at that moment but that I absolutely had to. I followed her upstairs with the wife of another one of the guys, and when we found the drunk woman, I lit into her about her alcoholism. As I walked upstairs, I had thought, *Are you really going to do this?* A "dumbass alert" rang vaguely in my head, but I ignored it. I countered that clanging bell with the thought, *You have to say hard things to people who need to hear them.*

I'm sure that this was the moment when Sam thought, *Okay, I'm canceling all of the dinner parties we have on the calendar. I cannot face this again.* She did not say this, of course. Easygoing people will never do that. She bit her lip and smiled. She pretended everything was as okay as she could and made the best of a horrible situation. Easygoing people don't say anything until you have pushed them into a corner and they're ready to die. The most important thing for them is that everybody gets along.

If you could ask Sam about that night now, she would probably say, "He had no idea how much he was upsetting me. He was upsetting a lot of other people, too." As I've said, Sam epitomizes all the things that you want in a partner: she is compassionate and caring and interested in whatever you're going through. And this beautiful woman with the sparkling personality had to sit next to me, listening to me talking to people about things that were grating on them. She could see that I was annoying the other guests and that they were trying their best to be hospitable. They tried not to offend me. They were basically trying to "manage the moron," Sam realized, and then, a moment later, she must have thought, *Wait a minute, I'm married to the moron.*

RECONNAISSANCE

I did not recognize that I was upsetting her because I hadn't done enough Reconnaissance to even know that she was an Easygoing person, much less appreciate the values of an Easygoing person. I did not recognize Sam's nature until it was too late to assemble a solid Target Package. Reading a book such as Florence Littauer's *Your*

Personality Tree is a good first step in understanding these four value systems.

Once I understood Sam's Easygoing personality value system, I came to appreciate that the most important thing for her is that everybody is getting along. Typically, that means she would rather eat glass than deal with conflict. Her parents were Easygoing and took a live-and-let-live attitude toward life. Sam took on their belief system, and so, if people were coming over to the house, in her mind, it needed to be a relaxed party where everyone was going to have a good time.

Sam loved those moments at home when everything was relaxed and the prevailing feeling was live-and-let-live. This was her programming: the pattern of attitudes, beliefs, and values—most of them subconscious—that each of us inherits during our first ten years. (We inherit this programming as children by either accepting or rejecting the programming of our parents—but I'll discuss that in more detail later on.) In the home where I was raised, on the other hand, conflict was the norm. We fought about most things. This was part of my programming. In every situation, my motivation was to stand and duke it out—the exact opposite of everything Sam valued most. Add to this the fact that I was a reformed born-again Christian married to a Jewish agnostic, and you can imagine the seeds of conflict that were germinating on evenings like the one I described.

> This was her programming: the pattern of attitudes, beliefs, and values—most of them subconscious—that each of us inherits during our first ten years.

Here's the point: we all inherit programming; we have no control over the programming we receive, and there isn't a "right" or a "wrong" program. People's programs are never their fault. These are the ingredients that go into making you before you have an independent thought in your head or a goal of your own. Programming is exactly that—a fixed set of brain instructions that, in effect, takes you over and governs your behavior when you least expect throughout your adult life. Sam and I had programs that were at odds with each other, but this did not mean either of us was in the wrong.

With the benefit of hindsight, I am able to analyze many examples of programming that played out in my marriage. For instance, I became an impossible religious nut-job, and Sam couldn't handle it, and so she left. We got divorced. One quick pattern behind this is that Sam's mum, Wendy, also married a guy who was relatively religious. She decided she didn't love him, and she left. Sam was, in a sense, following that programming when she left me and went back to Australia.

> Programming is exactly that—a fixed set of brain instructions that, in effect, takes you over and governs your behavior when you least expect throughout your adult life.

Sam's dad provided another program that affected her relationship with me. He divorced his first wife and brought two children from that marriage into his new marriage to Wendy, Sam's mother. Sam's family moved around the Pacific Rim a lot while she was growing up—Bangkok, Indonesia, Kuala Lumpur. Her father had a strained relationship with the children from the first marriage, and at some point, one of his sons came to live with his dad and new wife Wendy. The new arrangement became too stressful for Wendy, and she sent his son back to his mother in Australia. Jump to present time: Sam divorces me. She moves in with a guy who has two kids.

Those children are coming over to the house frequently, and she soon arrives at a place where she can't be around his children, because it's too stressful for her. There's absolutely nothing wrong with what's happening here—it's not her fault . . . it's just the programming playing out. This is the kind of High-Resolution Intelligence I should have been gathering in order to understand and save my marriage, but I didn't take the time to understand the dynamics at work back then.

Let's look at another example of such programs, one from my mother's life. My mother's biological mother died shortly after she was born. Her father married again to a woman with eight kids, and after the families were combined, at least one of her stepbrothers molested her.

Fast-forward to my childhood: when I turned ten, for no apparent reason, my mother suddenly rejected me emotionally. Based on the stories I've heard, this was roughly the age of the stepbrother when he molested my mother. When I turned ten, I was transformed into my mother's enemy. She did not consciously abandon me. It was as if she'd been hypnotized and a trigger was pulled. Mom couldn't help being influenced by her past. As her son, at ten years old, I was no longer trusted—not because I was molesting anyone but because my mom couldn't control—wasn't even aware of—a program that said she was not safe with a boy my age. The program simply took over my mother.

All I wanted was my mother's affection, which is vital for a child of that age. If you don't get it, there are side effects to reckon with. I spent my life longing for the affection I never received as a boy. I married Sam and got affection from her, but instead of being normal in this area, I was quite needy. Believe me, there is nothing more irritating to a woman than a needy man.

Interestingly, this ties back to another facet of my mother's programming. In her home, the pattern that she was mandated to adopt was that they were making "the image" of a perfect family. There could be no complaining, no criticism or suggestions that things were not right. It wasn't tolerated. My mom could not utter anything that even resembled a complaint to her dad or stepmother. Many of those family members—and my mother—had valid things to say about a family situation that was unhealthy in certain ways, but in her family, my mom was required to keep the surface smooth and pretend everything was fine. They kept a very clean house and did their best to pretend that everything was all right.

Because my mother grew up believing she had to act like everything was fine, I grew up oblivious to what a woman's needs might be. My parents would yell at me if I complained. I was being programmed to yell about stuff in order to be heard, and I imposed the same programming on Sam: "You're going to pretend everything is okay, or I'm going to yell at you." In my neediness, I was programmed to believe that she was supposed to meet these demands of mine, but she wasn't. I was the victim, and that made me quite needy emotionally.

ACTIONS-ON PLAN

Consider this in your own relationship with your wife. If you have been thinking about her as you read this chapter, then you have probably already identified one if not several things your wife does or attitudes she has that come from her childhood programming. For many reasons, these programs are important to recognize. For starters, understanding programming takes blame out of the equation. Programs are inherited, so they are no one's fault. Identifying programming also helps you to assemble a Target Package, and when you engage in Direct-Action Operations, it will give you the ability to understand and accept her attitudes, beliefs, or behaviors that you might have considered unreasonable. Considering the context of your wife's childhood and your own opens the door for compassion and understanding rather than judgment.

I should point out here that people receive programs in two ways. One I already discussed, and that's direct inheritance. If you saw your parents doing something that didn't bother you at all—there were no red flags, there were no moments where you thought the behavior was "a little off," then the chances are almost 100 percent that you are reproducing that program today, as naturally and thoughtlessly as you learned to brush your teeth and tie your shoes. Do you ever catch yourself saying something that your mom or dad said? This is a classic example of an inherited program.

The second way that you can inherit a program is by reacting against your parents' programming. If you saw them doing something that you don't agree with, it's as if you had antivirus software running in your brain. Let's say your parents were big screamers around the house, and you couldn't stand their screaming. You detested it with every fiber of your being. The odds are good that you bucked that programming and created another in its place. This does not mean that you necessarily gave yourself a healthy program. It might mean simply that, because you hate screaming, you decided to be very quiet. If you got to the point where you were so quiet that you didn't talk to anyone in your home, there was no balance there. In this case, the antivirus might have protected you from the yelling program but created another program equally problematic.

The bulk of programming is given to us before the age of ten. These are the "formative years," and we call them that because the synaptic connectors in the brain are much more flexible then. This does not mean that your brain synapses can't be broken free or that programming can't be changed after the age of ten, but the process requires more effort on your part.

Understanding how programs work can make you aware of potential fractures in your marriage and provide intel. Ignoring them will certainly lead to trouble. This might sound insane, but it's true. You can be the most talented man on the planet, and your wife might adore you, but if she is comfortable in chaos, then your orderly way of life will conflict with your chaos-loving woman, and a life without the chaos of her childhood home could become very uncomfortable for her. If she is also the child of divorce and she has been trying to get you to take her childhood pain away, she has the programming that requires her to leave you when there are persistent signs of trouble. You might actually have to allow her the chaos she needs to feel safe in some situations. This might become part of your Target Package, something you pursue in Direct-Action Operations.

RECONNAISSANCE

Programs lead to conflict, and understanding them can help us to reduce conflict and avoid arguing over the many things partners approach differently. Author Larry Bilotta describes fourteen issues that couples fight about most often. Explore this list as you think about your own programming, and consider how they are affecting your relationship:

1.   **Willpower.** In every home, one partner is more aggressive than the other, sometimes much more aggressive, and the other partner often feels like he or she is being bulldozed. In my childhood home, for instance, my mom ran the show.

Mom said how everything would go, and we all had to follow. It didn't matter that, overall, my father was a much more levelheaded person; my mom was clearly dominant.

2.   **Affection.** "Purpose" kids grow up with a high degree of safety and security, utterly confident that they are loved. "Chaos" kids grow up with neglect and abuse and very little confidence that they are loved. We all exist somewhere on this continuum. If purpose is a ten and chaos is a zero, where were you raised? My dad remembers at the age of five hating his father, and there was clearly neglect and abuse in my mom's house. As a result, my parents showed love and affection in childish ways. We had fun, but there was no real understanding of how to display unconditional love in a healthy way.

3.   **TV.** One partner always watches more TV, and sometimes it's a mechanism for avoidance. My dad lived in front of the TV and books because he needed an escape from the life he didn't want but signed up for. You can imagine the problems this might have caused when we kids were struggling with his wife's—our mom's—attempt to keep herself sane as her destructive childhood pushed her into inner turmoil. If you're glued to the TV, you might feel you have a great relationship with fun-loving people onscreen, but you're not part of your family.

4.   **Money.** Most couples immediately recognize money as a major source of conflict—often it tops the list for those who are young and struggling. Some are good with it, and some aren't. For some, it becomes an extreme obsession— the object of life—while others give it so little thought that

they put themselves and their families in constant financial risk. Finding the right balance here is important, especially considering your wife definitely has a need for financial security.

5. **Money in the Bank.** Like saving money, investing can be a source of contention. I already related my ill-fated investment in an African farm venture and the impact it had on my marriage. In my mom's house when she was growing up, all money had to be spent on the family, and so in my house growing up, all the money was spent on us. Get a dollar, spend a dollar was the program. So much for rainy days. What program did you receive regarding investment?

6. **Giving.** We've all seen it: one person in the house is Santa Claus and wants to give everything to everyone, while the other wants to save for some goal. My parents lavished gifts on others and us, and I did the same in my marriage. Sam did not appreciate my big heartedness. "I know that you want to be seen as the guy who's giving here," she often said, but what she didn't say, and what I should have heard was, "What about me and the kids?"

7. **Fighting.** For some people, shouting is quite normal, and one partner can become frustrated by the mouse-like personality who can't speak his or her mind. Others hate yelling more than anything and find raised voices completely obnoxious. In my home growing up, yelling was a good way to communicate that you were unhappy. This was not the case in Sam's house, and that disparity caused a great deal of discomfort for her.

8. **Talk.** How much is enough in a relationship? Can there be too much talking? One of you will always want to communicate more than the other. If an Easygoing person tells you "I love you" one time, they might feel like they never need to say it again. For them, efficiency is the priority, and being emotional is way down their list. But if your wife comes from a different place, she might need to talk about such feelings every day. In my childhood home, efforts to communicate were tense because they were riddled with the emotional land mines of what could or should be said.

9. **Listening.** Some are excellent at listening, and others need to work on it. Having one partner who is a great listener while the other only hears what they want to hear is bound to cause trouble. If someone wanted to express an idea in my house and my mom found it to be threatening or disagreed with it, there would be a price to pay if the conversation continued.

10. **Sensitivity.** If your childhood programming requires you to be highly sensitive to the needs of others and your wife's programming does not, there will likely be conflict. My parents, for example, tried but weren't very good at being sensitive to other personalities in the home. I was the only one who had the Joyful personality type. My sister was Easygoing, and my mother and father were also Easygoing, so they had a connection. There is a big difference between an Easygoing person raised in a chaos home and an Easygoing person raised in a cherished environment. My mom and dad yelled to communicate, yet they were both

Easygoing people. There is no disparity here. When a person has been pushed past their limits, that person who is normally peaceful can justify acting horribly.

11. **Relatives.** In my childhood family, time with relatives was a high priority. In Sam's childhood family, friends replaced relatives. She wondered why I spent so much energy attempting to be close to difficult relatives while pretending everything was okay. I was simply living according to my programming.

12. **Self-Worth**. If one spouse feels deserving of expensive champagne and the other feels worthy of no more than a light beer, that disconnect can create problems. Conflicts about money can rise at both extremes. Spouses with low self-image might feel undeserving of fine things and uncomfortable when their spouses buy expensive things they believe they themselves deserve. Low self-esteem often conflicts with high self-esteem, to the detriment of both.

13. **Marriage.** Couples usually have very different expectations of what their roles should be in marriage. Subconsciously, a man could easily expect his wife to value what his own mother valued. He could resent his wife if she varied too much from his mother's values. By contrast, his wife could subconsciously expect her husband to emulate her father's best qualities, while she defends herself from attitudes and actions of her husband that may mirror her father's worst qualities. Similarly, imagine you grew up without a dad at home because he was always working. As a result of that experience, you would be programmed to believe that the

mom should be running the house and you have no part in that aspect of family life.

14. **Belief.** In my childhood home, faith was a bulldozer, but in Sam's, there was not much religion: in her home, faith was "live and let live." These dramatically opposite views caused serious conflict when I returned to religion, became a born-again Christian, and tried to force it on her. I tried to force it on our kids, too, and it is often when children enter the picture that tensions over religion rise to the surface.

Here is a good rule of thumb: if your marriage is struggling, and you find at least six things on this list that you and your wife might agree on, then you have a good foundation for establishing a way forward, a common ground to build on. All is not lost if you *don't* find at least six things to agree on, but you need help, I promise you. If you are clearly aware of which issues ignite each of your childhood programs, then you can do some soul searching and begin to recognize the programs so that you can start talking about them openly. Read the fourteen-item list and identify the issues where you could benefit from a better program. This can become part of your Target Package. If, for instance, you're yelling at your kids a lot, part of your Direct-Action Operations might include taking some parenting classes. Make sure you get your wife's acceptance before you jump into any plan you believe is a good idea. Your life will be much more enjoyable. Making this sort of effort on your own will earn you major points with her, while also helping you become a better father and husband.

PROGRAMMING VIGNETTE

In January 2008, I became the 2IC (second in charge) of the Naval Special Warfare Prep School at Naval Station Great Lakes in Lake County, Illinois. Great Lakes is home of the US Navy's only boot camp and several technical schools charged with training sailors to work in the fleet. Admiral Lotring, the ranking officer, was ordered to help Naval Special Warfare open a prep school there. The admiral took great delight in calling this SEAL project "preschool"—because it happened before SEAL candidates went to Basic Underwater Demolition School (BUD/S) in Coronado, California.

The prep school is dramatically different from BUD/S. It consists of several civilian coaches who are there to inspire, encourage, and build upon whatever physical and mental capacity a candidate might have. An attrition rate of 80 percent in SEAL training prompted the new attempt to better prepare candidates before they face the rigors of what is arguably the hardest military training on the planet today. SEAL candidates attend classes ranging from physical maintenance (to keep their bodies healthy and ready for the next day of training) to nutrition and mental toughness.

I had a firm grasp of mental programming at this point, and I understood that the SEAL teams were full of guys who had "no-quit" programming. A no-quit program in someone happens before they turn ten, and one of their parents lived it or gave it to their child on purpose.

Despite the 80 percent historical attrition rate at BUD/S, no one ever will admit that he's the guy who will quit. It's actually surprisingly easy to identify who will drop out, despite the sure answer all SEAL candidates give.

Back in March 1992, I and some 237 people started in BUD/S Class 184. In October 1992, forty-two people graduated, seventeen of us from that original Class 184. The others quit, rolled into another class, or rolled out.

Programs, as I said, are acquired before you turn ten. I learned about the no-quit program when I played football at eight years old: I was taught that I signed up for it, so I had to do it—even if I didn't like it.

Cut to the coldest waters on earth in Coronado, California, with SEALs sitting in the ocean being surf-tortured. I had crocodile tears and big snot bubbles coming out of my nose. I had an out-of-body experience, cursing, praying in all tongues. But my programming won. I couldn't leave. I had signed up for this shit! I followed through because of my programming and graduated. I did not enjoy BUD/S at all, but I finished because I had signed up for it, and I was wired never to quit.

Years later, as the 2IC, I asked classes at the Naval Special Warfare Prep School: "How did your parents deal with adversity before you were ten? When they fought, what did they do? Did they quit and go to their separate rooms? Did they work it out? Did they get divorced? Did they stay from a sense of obligation but basically act like they hated each other? If they did get divorced, did you see your mom or dad have to dig deep to provide for those they loved?"

A "quit" program could happen for a kid simply because when little Johnny came home from soccer practice and told his parents that he didn't like soccer, his mom told his dad that she didn't think Johnny should have to go if he didn't want to. Dad sensed something was wrong, but he didn't want his wife mad at him, and he didn't want to hear Johnny crying, so he relented. Here is the issue: Johnny had a desire to play soccer, and when it got tough for a minute, he decided to leave. This seems like a nonissue, you think—except for this: Johnny is going to have many dreams in his life, and he is going to start out trying to accomplish those dreams. The program for him to sabotage those dreams is lurking. He is likely to go through a lot of his life pursuing dreams and constantly changing course because he quits on them. This is exactly what he is supposed to do, according to the programming he got before he turned ten.

Jim, a candidate in the prep school, was able to identify that he had weak programming and had the courage to approach me after class. We talked about things, but talk is like a frame on a house. It's not a house until it's all wired up, walls are in, and it's decorated and complete. Navy regulations mandate that students be treated a certain way, so sometimes talk is the only thing you can do. However, when a student gets in trouble, other measures can be taken under the umbrella of corrective action. Fortunately for all of us, Jim got in trouble, and no little trouble either. We had the right to kick Jim out of training. I wanted to try something else, though, and he was going to say yes to any idea that would allow him a chance to achieve his dream.

The basic physical scores you need to get into BUD/S are to complete a five-hundred-yard swim in twelve and a half minutes, forty-two push-ups in two minutes, fifty sit-ups in two minutes, six pull-ups with no time limit, and a one-and-a-half mile run in boots in eleven minutes. My sister can meet these standards, and if you achieve the minimum, those scores give you less than a 7 percent chance of succeeding in BUD/S. An 80 percent success rate, according to statistics based on graduates of SEAL training since 1963, looks like this: a five-hundred-yard swim in nine minutes, one hundred push-ups in two minutes, one hundred sit-ups in two minutes, twenty pull-ups with no time limit, and one and a half miles in eight minutes.

With this in mind, I did Jim a favor. I told Jim his Liberty (evening free time and weekends) would be secured (withheld) until he achieved standards that gave him an 80 percent chance of succeeding physically. I also added a subjective score to the weight training he was doing. Coaches scored every candidate every day in the weight room: zero, one, or two. If you get noticed slacking, you get a zero; if you get noticed crushing it, you get a two. If you don't get noticed, you get a one. Easy. I told Jim that in addition to the required standards that would get him to 80 percent, he needed four twos in weight training to free himself. Four weeks later, coaches confirmed that Jim had reached the highest physical standards. But he was lacking on the scores he needed in the weight room. Jim came into my office to discuss the weight training. By this time, he knew I wasn't actually punishing him at all. He knew I cared and that I genuinely wanted him to be successful.

He said he was working hard in the weight room, but the coaches just weren't giving him the twos. He asked if I would go watch to see if I could help him out.

Later that day, I walked into the weight room, and within fifteen minutes, the answer to why he wasn't getting the score became apparent: he was saving his energy—saving it for the rest of that day's workouts, the rest of the week, and the rest of his time in the prep school and BUD/S. He came to my office, and I told him he was holding back and why I thought he was doing so. He was astonished and confirmed that it was true, and he became discouraged. He was convinced he was screwed. He reasoned he wouldn't have the energy to perform for the week and succeed through all of training if he actually went all-out in the weight room.

I suggested he do a trial for a week to see if his thoughts were true or if he could still perform in other events after going 100 percent on the weights. He got all the twos he needed and was released from the mandate I had placed on him.

I saw Jim seven months later. It was his graduation, and I was at BUD/S in Coronado for the week. He introduced me to his mother. Both of them were proud beyond measure.

SEAL training isn't fair, but the enemy isn't fair, so the training is as brutal and warlike as we can make it, without actually going to war. Chances are high that your wife is not doing things that are fair at all. However, being a gentleman and understanding her programming—and understanding and appreciating the flamethrower of hell she has justifiable reasons to throw at you—is a great mind-set to adopt at this point. Assembling a Target Package for your marriage isn't easy, but following through with Direct-Action Operations requires persevering in the face of unimaginable suffering. Quelling the fires of hell and loving her while she's making moves to make another life without you, for instance, will test you beyond any pain I would ever wish on anyone. Refusing to allow the new guy in her life to crush you and making his presence a nonissue while you throw your hat in the ring again to win her heart won't be easy, but it is where you have to go if you want to come out of this victori-

> SEAL training isn't fair, but the enemy isn't fair, so the training is as brutal and warlike as we can make it, without actually going to war.

ous. She and your kids are worth the 100-percent effort you are going to have to put into this.

Just as our coaches didn't give Jim the twos he needed to succeed simply because they knew he wanted them, your wife isn't going to give you the twos you need to win her heart back unless you truly let go of all pride and dig all the way to hell to demand of yourself 100 percent and earn the prize you truly can't afford to lose.

EXECUTION ORDERS

Write down, on the middle of a blank piece of paper, the list of fourteen issues that couples fight about most often. Put your name on the left and her name on the right and create a short sentence that describes how you were programmed to deal with each of those items and how your wife was programmed to deal with those items. You will surely identify why friction happens simply because of the program each of you has. Give your wife her desires according to her programming, no matter how much it violates your programming— unless it is a matter of life and death and her programming will land you in jail.

CHAPTER 4

NAME YOUR ENEMY

You are getting help sabotaging your marriage.

Are you a good person?

Nearly everyone answers this question in the affirmative. Most require a little help with another, related question: Do you want good things for yourself and the people you love? Perhaps you've done some bad things or steered away from the path you wanted to follow. Since you want good things for yourself and others, you are essentially a good person.

It is a scientific fact that a positive thought and a negative thought can't occur in your head at the exact same moment. Skeptical? Try it.

Think of the worst thing that happened to you. Now, think of the best thing that happened. Try to think about those memories at the exact same moment. Can't be done.

This logic brings us to another question and ultimately, a conclusion. If you are a good person who wants good things for yourself and other people, and we have identified that negative and positive thoughts can't occur at the same time—then where do negative thoughts come from?

If a surgeon cuts you open, he will not find your hopes, dreams, and personality on display, because you are an invisible being living inside a physical "machine." Religious people might think I'm describing a "soul," a word that conjures something invisible, but even the nonreligious can appreciate the idea that the physical parts that make up the body of the person are not the entire person. There is an invisible part of you that science often calls "the ghost in the machine." Your hopes, dreams, and personality would not be found by the surgeon—yet aren't they the core of who you are?

Now, if you are an invisible being living inside a physical machine, is there a law that says you must fill the body from head to toe? How big is the "invisible" you? As an invisible being, do you have to fit in a certain space? Theoretically, you could be as big as your heart or fill your entire house, couldn't you? As an invisible being, you could be any size, fill any space.

Ask yourself another question: Do you ever get a "good vibe" from someone you meet for the first time? Whatever we call it, all of us have had the feeling: *I just really like that guy. I don't know why, but I get a good vibe.* And similarly, we sometimes get "bad vibes." You've seen this with a young child who walks up to an adult and instantly dislikes him. The child gets a bad vibe. Could it be that the invisible you is determining these vibes?

We started with the idea that you think of yourself as essentially good, but why is it so easy to be bad? It seems like there's some kind of invisible encourager that makes us gravitate toward bad things we don't want to do.

Being good takes work and concentration, and you must stay alert to be a good person. Being bad is the opposite. Being bad, insensitive, rude, offensive, and angry is easy and comes without any effort on your part. It's like you're being taken over. I'm sure you know the feeling.

Say you're a good person and want good things for yourself and others, yet you have bad thoughts that hold back your good intentions; you can hypothetically imagine that there is an "evil" presence in your mind—an entity completely separate from the good presence that makes up the invisible you. That evil presence is bent on doing wrong and counters the good you. You are fundamentally good, but that evil you is really revealing a "you" to others that isn't you at all.

This is not a new idea. Think about many of history's great authors who wrote on the idea of fighting one's inner demons. Remember all of the cartoons where we see an angel on one shoulder and the devil on the other? Maybe you've heard people say this phrase: "I don't know what it is, but I just don't feel like myself today." There is an "other" force that overcomes our natural goodness.

Everybody intuitively knows there's something in us that is not the "true" us. It has been written about and portrayed in books and movies and songs for centuries. Think of the phrases we use all the time: "I can't tell who she is anymore . . . I don't know what came over me . . . I don't know what got into me, but the next thing I knew I . . ."

Virtually all literature, art, and film portray this good versus evil idea, and our lives demonstrate it all the time. If good versus evil is at the center of so much, wouldn't it make sense that we must be made of the exact same stuff of good versus evil? Understanding and accepting these two forces is the first step to overcoming the negative force.

HIGH-RESOLUTION INTELLIGENCE

In the movie *Thunderheart*, Val Kilmer plays a government agent on an Indian reservation, and somebody questions what makes him tick. In response, he says that he has a "good wolf" and a "bad wolf" living inside him. The other man asks him which is stronger. He answers, "The one that I feed."

If you have been "feeding the bad wolf," as Val Kilmer put it, consider what happens when it comes to your marriage and your kids. If the Bad Wolf is taking you over and doing bad things to them, have you been feeding the Bad Wolf without even realizing it?

You might conclude that if there is a dark force inside that you can't control, then you can blame that entity for anything negative that comes out of your behavior. It wasn't my fault—it was my "bad self." But let's say your dog gets away from you and bites a child. You are taken to court. Who does the judge punish, you or your dog? The dog owner pays the penalty for the actions of the dog.

As a Navy SEAL, no one understands better than I do how important it is to give a name and a face to the enemy. This is key to every war effort—and remember, we are approaching the fight to save your marriage as if it is a complex military operation.

Consider the historical precedents for the utility of putting a name and a face on evil. During World War II, evil had a name and a face. Adolph Hitler represented all that was evil, and the free world united against that clear enemy and won the war. By contrast, in Vietnam, the enemy was an ideology called communism. There was no name or face for that enemy, and the war tore the US apart because the population was divided. People were not sure who the enemy was, and consequently, they lost their resolve to win.

Although the metaphor of the Bad Wolf is helpful, there is another that I like even more: Freddy Kreuger from the *Nightmare on Elm Street* movies. The character of Freddy Krueger is a perfect characterization of evil because he is ugly, diabolical, and wants to separate you from those you love. He wants to destroy everything that is valuable to you. He invades the dream of your life and turns it into a nightmare. He isn't some nameless evil. He is Freddy, and his name says it all.

Anyone who's gone through divorce will tell you that divorce is destruction: the Bad Wolf always wins. Destruction might be a metaphor here, but it could be literal. According to *Between Two Worlds: The Inner Lives of Children of Divorce* by Elizabeth Marquardt, the children of broken homes are almost twice as likely to attempt suicide as children of intact homes. They are also more likely to drop out of high school, report problems with their peers, experience anxiety, and suffer a host of other problems.

Calling the dark force inside you Freddy might seem a little odd, but it gives a focus to the bad impulses within you. Once named, it can be defeated.

ACTIONS-ON PLAN

Your first action is to name your enemy.

I could list many more examples, but suffice it to say that it is vital to have a name and a face for the enemy. When I accepted this logic and realized there was something dark operating within me and convincing me to do terrible things, my reaction was anger. At first, my negative reaction to Freddy only compounded the "terrible things" I wanted to avoid. Freddy was winning, but I accepted that he existed in me, and I intended to defeat him.

It was as if Freddy Kruger was showing me a picture of what I wanted, then switching to a picture of what I could not have. Then, he would give me a kind of drug that made me feel good for a few seconds. It's as if he said, "Here, take this, and you'll solve this problem with your wife not cooperating with you. Get angry and show her you're in charge. That will feel good, too." Being naive, I took the drug and got angry, and it felt good. But there were enormous consequences for taking the anger drug. You take the drug because you believe that anger will fix what you think is broken, but you also drag into your life more anger from the one you attacked. That's a quick picture of living with your Bad Wolf.

I needed to resist that drug. I needed to say to myself that while it feels good getting angry and telling people off, there are long-lasting consequences to its use. I am continually making people hate me. I don't have the friends that I want, and if anger solves one problem short term, it creates ten more long term. This is why allowing Freddy to get you all worked up is such a trap. People want to stick him in a box, and they want to hate him, but if you watched the first *Nightmare on Elm Street* movie, the way the heroine beats him is not with anger. She doesn't react in an emotionally negative way. Instead, she shines a mirror back on him, and the mirror view of his own image destroys him. This mirror concept will be discussed later on in the book, but it is one of the most important keys to success in realizing a better personal life and relationship with those you love most.

Let's look at an example that has nothing to do with marriage. Cancer survivors will tell you that their attitude had everything to do with making it, and many will say that they had to love and respect the cancer in order to free themselves from it. *I had to appreciate what Freddy Kruger did for me, which would eventually make me a more loving person.* Some survivors believe that chemo and radiation were important, but again and again, they return to their new attitude and becoming more loving people as the key that changed the course of the disease. I am not pitching the idea that you should hate Freddy Kruger. I am merely saying that he exists—the Bad Wolf is real—and conflict feeds him.

The job of killing off your Bad Wolf goes back to my earlier concept that two thoughts, one positive and the other negative, can't exist at the same time in the same person. So when you decide to create positive thoughts, such as *I am worthy, I am happy, I am kind, I listen, I am heard, I am appreciated, I am accepted, I am connected,* you are focusing all your energy on ideas that will suffocate your Bad Wolf. He cannot survive in a positive thought environment.

What are the things that you didn't receive in your past, and how are they still creating negative feelings all these years later? How can you make sure they don't keep coming back like Bill Murray in the movie *Groundhog Day*? How can you avoid feeding the Bad Wolf, no matter how justifiable your negative feelings might be?

Here's another way I used to feed the Bad Wolf and let him win—and just like you, I was completely unaware of it. After I decided to turn over a new leaf, to be a loyal husband and go back to religion, I started attending a Messianic synagogue called Beth Messiah, in Virginia Beach. There are many beautiful things about the Jewish religion. I had read the Bible multiple times, but until I attended this synagogue, I'd never seen the Old Testament come alive. I had never understood why we celebrated this thing called Easter instead of Passover as explained in the Bible, but Messianic Judaism gave a beautiful picture of the Christian faith as it probably existed in the first century.

One of the main goals of this religion is to recruit Jews and convince them that Jesus, *Yeshua Bin David*, the Jewish Messiah, does exist. If Sam, this Jewish-agnostic girl, came to the synagogue, there was a sense of urgency on the part of the congregation to get her to believe. When she showed up, it was game on, which put a lot of pressure on her, especially since she'd grown up in a house without much religious tradition.

I can appreciate this context now, but back then, I would wake up on any given Shabbat and say, "Okay, let's go to Temple." Sometimes Sam would go, but at some point she decided that it was too much for her. My attempts to change her mind put her in a difficult spot. Remember, she's an Easygoing person, and she wants everyone to get along. She did not want to go and face the pressure at the synagogue, but she didn't want to upset me, either.

Inevitably, I would go on my own and pretend that I wasn't upset—but I was. I would take the drug of anger. I was angry about her not going, and she was feeling that energy. I was a good person trying to do a good thing—keep my family together and bring them all to church. But then Freddy Kruger entered and showed me the picture of the thing I wanted—my family sitting in synagogue and worshipping together—and then he showed me the image of this person who didn't want to go. "She's in the wrong," Freddy would say, "because it clearly states in the Bible that you need to be going to church every Sabbath or Sunday."

Tension built until Sam finally couldn't do it anymore, and an argument erupted. Replace this issue—religion—with any hot-button issue that comes up between you and your wife. The cycle is the same. Freddy gets you to take the drug of anger until the situation builds to an argument. Afterward, you might see the issue clearly for what it is, but then he gives you the drug of guilt. This is another terrible Freddy drug because it punishes you until you react against it, and Freddy wins again. "Fine," Freddy says, "that's enough guilt. Let's get angry again! She should be doing this or that, and she isn't!"

This is a nasty cycle of emotional drugs that you must leave if you want to be a man who is calm and safe to be around. How do you do this?

RECONNAISSANCE

In order to beat Freddy, you must have a sense of how he works. The following analogy will give you insight into how your Freddy manipulates you. First, let's think about *where* he is manipulating you. The place where all this manipulation happens is your internal television set. We all know this place as your imagination. The problem is your Bad Wolf can take over your imagination, decide what channel it wants to watch, and play that on repeat in your head for as long as it wants.

Your nervous system does not care what channel is playing on your imagination television. It knows only that it is getting a feeling from it. Your Freddy tries to label bad things you're looking at as bad, and he attempts to label good things you're looking at as bad as well. He does this through a little organ in your brain called the amygdala. The role of the amygdala is well explained in the book *Emotional Intelligence* by Daniel Goleman.

It was Goleman who originally explained that the amygdala's job is to warn you of danger and that it is not a very accurate device. It scans your situation and compares what you are experiencing with something that happened in the past. It is your Freddy that pulls up negative images from the past and matches them to your current situation. At that moment, your job is to take whatever situation you're facing and overlay it with something positive.

Freddy doesn't like that at all.

This is what Viktor Frankl, the Austrian neurologist and psychiatrist who survived the Holocaust, explained in his book *Man's Search for Meaning*. Frankl wrote from his perspective as a clinical psychiatrist about his fellow inmates in the Nazi concentration camp. Frankl determined that good meaning could be found in even the most horrific and dehumanizing situations, and that love—man's highest purpose—can exist even there. According to Frankl, the people who did the best in the concentration camp found love in their hearts even in this deadly situation. They managed to love their fellow inmates and themselves and sometimes even their Nazi guards.

They chose not to allow anything to derail them, no matter how terrifying or physically painful. They either gave events no meaning or found positive meaning and tried to love the person on the other side of the act. The story of another Holocaust survivor provides a second good example. After watching Nazis slaughter his family, this man did not get angry but vowed that he would never hate again. If you think avoiding anger and hate by changing your imagination's channel will be difficult for you, consider this man's extreme situation. He managed to avoid hate despite horrific circumstances, and when the allies came, he was in much better health than those around him. Some said he looked as if the war had hardly touched him. He'd been protected by love; his method of survival was to demonstrate genuine compassion and care for anyone who was in his presence—Jew and Nazi alike.

HIGH-RESOLUTION INTELLIGENCE

We'll close out this chapter with another story, an ancient one that drives home the idea of mastering your imagination television and not letting Freddy get the upper hand.

A Chinese farmer lived with his son, raising horses and vegetables. One day, the son broke his leg. The townspeople expressed their sadness, saying, "You must be very distressed about your son's leg, for now you must work the farm alone."

The farmer replied, "Maybe, maybe not."

As the son's leg healed, the emperor declared war and drafted all the young men for battle, but the farmer's son was rejected because of his broken leg. The townspeople heard about this and said to the farmer, "You must be very happy about your son's condition, for it saved him from going to war!"

The farmer replied, "Maybe, maybe not."

As the son limped around the farm doing his chores, he accidentally left the gate open one night and all one hundred horses ran away. The next day, people from the town came out and said to the farmer, "It is so sad that you lost all your livestock. Now you will make very little money."

The farmer replied, "Maybe, maybe not."

News came to the farmer that the war was over and that the emperor had decided to hold a lottery and redistribute all the livestock. The farmer drew the long straw and received five hundred horses. The townspeople rallied around him and said, "You must be very happy now that you have prospered so richly!"

Guess what the farmer said?

He knew something that few people understand: events have no meaning except the meaning you (or the enemy inside of you) give them. The Chinese farmer decided that he would not let his emotions carry him high or low. He simply controlled what he could, stayed calm, and let events take their course. He did not let events control him.

With this idea in mind, you can actually choose to label all events that show up in your life as "good." By deciding the meaning of every event and calling it "good," you will be changing the vibration of your situation instead of letting the situation (governed by Freddy) dictate how you respond.

EXECUTION ORDERS

Feel the difference between your good self and your Freddy. Whenever you are calm, cool, and collected—you are you. Whenever you are burning, irritated, or feeling unappreciated and disrespected, your Freddy has hijacked you, and he will justify anger as a response. But anger will simply bring more anger. Find a way to regain control while staying calm, cool, and collected. Realize that your wife, too, is probably at battle with her inner Freddy. Choose to love her *and* her Freddy. Once you do this—and get yourself out of the negative-energy trap—the anger in her will quickly dissipate.

CHAPTER 5

CLEAN THE MESS

*Take 100 percent responsibility—even
for things that aren't your fault.*

I described how my mother rejected me emotionally when I turned ten because this was the age her stepbrother was when he molested her. Mom didn't trust me. I was abandoned and denied affection not because of anything I'd done but because of my mother's past—because of a program repeating itself.

How would I deal with this situation today in light of what I've explained so far? Knowing everything I know now, if I could go back in time to talk to ten-year-old Darek, I would ask, "Okay, Darek, how does it feel to believe that your mom has abandoned you?"

The ten-year-old would say, "It's terrible."

My response would be, "Okay, I appreciate that. Our emotions tell us a lot. If we feel bad about a certain situation, that means we're not actually looking at the situation with our highest self. Let's see what would happen if you thought about the idea that your mom was not abandoning you. Instead, your mom is hurting over something that happened to her. Then how would you feel?"

"Well," young Darek would say, "I guess I would start feeling bad for her instead of feeling bad for me."

"Good point, but let's talk through this possibility. Paint me a picture of what it looks like when your mom cares for you that might help her know she's as understood as she is going to be from a ten-year-old."

He might say, "Well, my mom would talk to me and say something like, 'Look, I'm trying to figure some things out now. Your sister is seven and you're ten. I'm feeling bad about some things that happened to me when I was a little girl, and I'm scared you might do to her what my brother(s) did to me. I don't know how not to be scared.'"

"How do you feel after imagining this, Darek?"

"I don't feel so abandoned anymore. My feeling now is, okay, Mom, what can I do to let you know that you're safe? Now we're having a good conversation, and I don't feel abandoned at all. This feels much better."

The news is full of people violating others and countries doing something horrible to another country. Shouldn't we all be outraged? We get together to blog about it and talk about it and discuss how screwed up this person or that person is. Is this sort of talk going to change that person? No, it never does.

In my conversation with my younger self, the effort to talk the situation through is something I did internally, and it had a powerful effect. Believe it or not, going through the process again by writing about it just now created good energy and left me feeling like I was emotionally connected to my mother. She appreciated me. She heard me. I heard her, and I understood her situation. Just thinking about that now actually changes the energy within me.

Best of all, changing the energy contained in painful past moments ultimately changes everything in your life. That's because you change the meaning, which changes the movie playing in your imagination. Your imagination runs your nervous system, and your nervous system creates your feelings. You could choose to spend your life angry about everything that you don't have, or you could create good meaning about what's in front of you right now and have that wave of good energy continue endlessly.

There is a system you can use to identify when you are feeling bad and help get yourself to a place where you're feeling better. Look at an unpleasant event—perhaps it's your wife taking away all her affection. It's a situation that makes you feel rejected.

The imagination television analogy is helpful here because you can essentially "change the channel" and place yourself in another movie, one where your girl is being affectionate rather than withhold-ing, or she is listening instead of yelling. You can change the energy. It's hard if not impossible to jump right to what you "wish" you had when you have so much momentum focused on what you don't have. I totally understand, so let's slow the momentum before getting too frustrated at not being able to immediately flip the switch.

HIGH-RESOLUTION INTELLIGENCE

The first part of this slowing process is identification. Once you identify that an event is happening that you don't like, it is time to consider this next story:

An old janitor was sweeping the steps of an apartment building. Through an open window, he heard a baby screaming. A young woman stomped out onto the steps of the building to get relief from her noisy baby. The janitor heard her complaining about how much she hated her life. He turned his attention to the young woman and said, "You're saying that because you don't know about the clay box."

Now, both confused and interested, the woman replied, "What's a clay box?"

"Why tell you when I can show you?" he said.

The janitor went into the building and brought out a wooden box. He sat down beside her on the steps and opened the box to reveal three lumps of clay about the size of limes. One was gray, the second one red, and the third one green.

"Take that gray lump of clay. Using this toothpick, I want you to make it into a happy puppy. Do the best you can," he said. The girl quickly manipulated the clay into a silly puppy face, and she giggled like a schoolgirl. "How did that make you feel?" the janitor asked.

"It made me feel silly and happy," the girl replied.

"Now take that red clay and make it into a grumpy old man." The girl quickly got into the task and, using the toothpick, created a snarly face with a bad attitude. "Now how does that face make you feel?" the janitor asked.

"It sure doesn't make me feel good," the girl quickly replied.

"Then take that green clay, and I want you to make an evil monster," the janitor said in all seriousness.

The girl began work on the assignment but dropped the green clay back into the box and said, "I can't do it."

"Why not?" the janitor said.

"It just makes me feel bad. I don't want to make an evil monster."

"Can I tell you what you just did?" the janitor asked. "You just became a creator, and when you created something, you felt something. When you created something happy, you felt happy. When you created something grumpy, you felt down. When you attempted to create something evil, you didn't even want to finish," the janitor explained.

"So what are you saying?" the girl asked impatiently.

"Your life is a clay box, is what I'm saying," the janitor replied solemnly. "If you don't create the clay of your life, it will turn into something that disappoints you and even makes you angry. If you choose to mold your clay into anything you want, then your life will become just like it."

Before the girl could really react to the message, the

janitor picked up the box and turned toward the building. Suddenly, he glanced back at the young woman and said "Twenty years ago, I was the janitor of this place. Because of that clay box, now I own it."

Now, return to your best memory. Remember what you felt at that moment. Store that feeling.

If you want to change your life and your marriage, you're going to need to mold your feelings into what you want them to be. Remember that your nervous system is composed of millions of nerves that only care about what plays on your imagination television. You might be molding a picture of what you don't want, but you can choose, just like the sculptor does, to mold it into something beautiful.

All sculptors begin with a lump of clay and a vision of what it could be. They don't sit and complain about the clay that lies in front of them. They keep working on the clay, molding it into the image of whatever channel is playing in their imagination. That's exactly what you will be doing. Molding the clay of your life is actually molding your imagination into what you want your life to be.

A good application of this molding-clay idea is an exercise that involves creating a story from your best memory. This should be a specific and wonderful event that actually happened to you. I recommend that you actually write this memory down to make it powerful and vivid. Every time you want to use this story, you should begin by saying, "You know what this reminds me of? It reminds me of the time . . ." This transition allows you to join the current event with your best memory or story. As an example of what a best memory is like, I'll share mine.

You know what this reminds me of? It reminds me of the time I was competing in the state championships in swimming in '91, at the Epic Center in Longmont, Colorado. I was about to swim the one-hundred-yard butterfly. Energy was just surging through the place, and it was surging through my body, too. I was nervous, but I was ready to swim.

The atmosphere in the building was electric. The pool looked like blue crystal that was streaked with oil from swimmers' bodies (there was a bottle of baby oil in front of every lane). My coach stood next to me. This was the culmination of three hard years of training. Though I knew he was anxious about how I would do, my coach was quite calm. Over the PA system, they called finalists in the one hundred butterfly to the blocks.

I could hear my parents and teammates cheering for me as I made my way to the blocks. I scraped my arms to get all the dead skin off and better feel the water. I wanted to feel its texture. I rinsed my goggles in the water after spitting in them to ensure they wouldn't fog. I could smell chlorine and baby oil. My body was glistening in the stuff. I climbed on the block.

"Swimmers, take your mark." Bang.

I hit the water hard and fast. The first two lengths were done before I knew it. On the third length, my body began to scream. I could hear my dad yelling, "Go, Darek! Go!" I was neck-and-neck with the guy in the next lane. My lungs were burning. We hit the third wall. My coach was screaming, "Go, Darek!" I pushed in the water with everything I had. I could hear my team, my coach, and my dad way up in the stands: "Go, Darek, Go!"

My arms burned. My legs were exploding. I didn't care. I pushed them to the limits. I reached and pulled all the water I could grab to propel me to the finish. I hit the wall and looked at the scoreboard: "I won! I won!" I climbed out of the pool. My coach handed me a towel and tapped me on the shoulder. My dad looked at me like he knew I was going to make it in life. He was so proud. It was awesome. I felt like I could do anything.

Having this sort of special, positive memory at your command is the key to part two: changing the channel.

If you're feeling terrible, you can and must change the channel. When you've gotten this far using your best memory and used your clay box, check your feelings again and realize that you feel very different than you did before. That's because your imagination really does control how you feel. You have taken control of your imagination and, thus, your feelings. If you're like most people, you've done it for the very first time.

Anger, worry, resentment, doubt, and fear never produce happiness. Thinking that they can is the equivalent of planting a weed and expecting an apple tree. If you plant anger, an anger tree is going to grow. Accept the fact that anger or any of the other popular negative emotions will never give you what you want.

ACTIONS-ON PLAN

Think about one of your programs that is telling you to behave badly. Let's say it's something like, "I am worthless." This is a program. Programs can be changed. Let's do that now.

On a full page, draw a large box and draw a small box below it. The large box will be your new software program. The small box will be your old software program. We know software programs can be rewritten, and that belief about software programs is already in our brains. Now write the old program in the small box, "I am worthless," and label it Version 1.0. We know software uses numbers to keep track of the latest program version. Now, in the big box above, print the new program you want to install in your brain: "I am valuable, and I treat others with respect." In the big box, give this new software a high version number, showing that this is improved software. Label the big box VERSION 12.0, with the title of the new program written in BOLD LETTERS.

To remove that old program from your brain, you must replace the old weak program with the newer, improved program. Here's how to do it. First read the old box software name (I am worthless) and version number, then the new box software name (I am valuable, and I treat others with respect) and version number. Read back and forth by glancing between the two images quickly for about thirty seconds. Your brain is getting the message that the old software must be removed and the new software must replace it. Your brain knows to do that because of two ideas you put on your page. First, you made a large box above and a small box below. Your brain knows from past images that whatever is above and bigger is better and whatever is below and smaller is less valuable. Second, you put version numbers to the software programs. Your brain knows all about software version numbers. Now your neurons know what to do. Replace the small, low-version-number message with the big, high-version-number message. Your brain is flexible if you give it the right instructions. Now you can remove your old programs and replace them with better instructions. You'll need to do this exercise every single day for thirty days if you want to see a real change. Think of this as similar to the SEAL training I have described. Like the exercises that allow SEALs to tackle dangerous missions, this sort of exercise will improve your readiness for Mission Execution.

These new skills and tools will allow you to have completely different discussions with your intimate partner, talks that previously might have ended in tears but now offer High-Resolution Intelligence. If you have been a tyrant, for instance, and you're in an argument with your wife, you will be able to suddenly change your whole attitude and engage in Direct-Action Operations: "I'm sorry about the way that I reacted there for a second. You obviously are upset about something. Tell me about it. I just want to get it right for you."

DIRECT-ACTION OPERATIONS

The strategies I've discussed for controlling your imagination will help you to build successful relationships and happiness in the present, but what about all the past traumas and tragedies you have suffered? If you're human and you made it through childhood, the odds are good that some negative things happened to you in the past, things that scarred you in some way and are still influencing your behavior today. How are you supposed to deal with the negative energy that those past traumas still create today?

At the start of this chapter, I discussed what I might say to the young version of me, if I could go back in time, to help that boy deal with the limited affection his mother gave. Even though literal time travel isn't an option, we can travel through time in our imagination. We can alter energy in the past moments when trauma was inflicted. In the story about young Darek, he came to the realization that whatever mistakes his mom made, she never meant to hurt him. Neither did your mom or dad. If you have kids, you know that you love them more than anything. You're doing the best you can, but sometimes your Freddy screws you up. Your kids will have to deal with those mistakes, just as you had to deal with the mistakes your parents' Freddies created.

For some readers, the following concept will be one of the more difficult ones in the book. Let's start with the idea that the tragedies that have occurred in your life up to now are not your fault. Your parents and their Freddies might have perpetrated some of the worst of them, but they're not your parents' fault either. It is possible for you to take responsibility for those tragedies and traumas and take control of them, even though you didn't cause them.

An analogy is helpful here. Imagine that you are a beautiful island, and one day, the Exxon Valdez is passing by. The captain screws up. He hits the shoals and dumps an oil slick on you. It's killing your plant life. It's killing your wildlife. It's turning you into an ugly island. You can be as mad as you want at the captain who caused this situation, but that does not give you what you want. You want to be a beautiful island again. The quicker that you take responsibility for that cleanup, the more enjoyable your island life is going to be.

> It is possible for you to take responsibility for those tragedies and traumas and take control of them, even though you didn't cause them.

RECONNAISSANCE

Another helpful illustration of this healing process can be found in the book *Zero Limits* by Joe Vitale and Dr. Ihaleakala Hew Len. Dr. Hew Len took over a psychiatric ward for the criminally insane at Hawaii State Hospital in the eighties. Few if any of the residents were expected to be freed ever or even to show slight improvement. Psychologists quit monthly, and the staff feared for their own safety. Dr. Hew Len did not see or treat a single patient, but within a few years, nearly every patient had been healed or released, and the ward was shut down.

How did he do it? He used the ancient Hawaiian art of *ho'oponopono*, a practice of reconciliation and forgiveness. The term literally means "to make right" and is defined by the *Hawaiian Dictionary* as a kind of "mental cleansing" through prayer, repentance, restitution, and forgiveness. Rather than using Western-style therapy or analysis or medications, Dr. Hew Len read the patients' files, poring over the horrific things that they had done, and as he did so, he identified in himself how he personally was responsible for the horrific acts they'd committed. He then uttered four statements in a process he called "cleansing."

He said, "I'm sorry. I love you. Please forgive me. Thank you."

His "apology" was done privately in his thoughts, and it had several facets. He genuinely reflected on his own life to find something he was personally sorry for, something bad he'd done or that had been done to him. He would then ask a higher power—divinity, God, the universe, however you see it—*How is this situation my responsibility? How am I responsible for this?* Whatever picture appeared to him, he would be genuinely apologetic for it. If the image was of somebody doing something bad to him, he would say that he was sorry, as if he'd done it himself. He also apologized from the inmate's perspective to his or her victims and then also to himself.

The process seems counterintuitive but can result in great healing. A lot of what I've talked about has to do with taking responsibility for your life—*all* of your life, even the things that are not your fault. As Dr. Hew Len explains it, everything you see, smell, touch, hear, etc., is your responsibility because it is part of your life. As I said earlier, situations aren't good or bad until you give them a meaning. Nothing in the world has meaning until you give it meaning, until you take full responsibility. In a sense, then, the entire world is your creation.

How might this work as part of the Direct-Action Operations that you will take to save your marriage? Here's an example: I'm sitting at the table with Sam and feeling self-righteous, talking about Christian matters. I'm repeating the name Jesus over and over every couple seconds just because I see it's making her mad. This is the one and only occasion Sam ever physically lashes out, and like a complete ass, I laugh at her instead of understanding how angry and hurt she must be as an Easygoing person to be pushed to that extreme. (To my great embarrassment, this example is all my fault. The lesson here is to not laugh or make things worse, but to use the moment to take responsibility.)

Using the method I've described, I might say, "Sam, I'm sorry that I pushed you to rage. I should have never done that. I love you. Please forgive me for being an idiot, for being a jackass, for goading you. Thank you for reacting the way you did to show me that I lost my control and created this situation." Next, in my imagination, I shift to Sam's point of view and I say to myself from her perspective: *Darek, I'm sorry I hit you. Please forgive me for not understanding that you're trying to be a loving husband. You just don't know how. I love you for everything that you are trying to do for our family. Thank you for showing me that I'm not as accepting of people as I want to be. I'll work on it and try to get better.* Remember this: doing what I'm describing makes you feel good. It is not about the other person. Sam—or whomever you apply this approach to—might never say that sentence. She never has to.

This is something you do personally, in your own head, something that feels good. Sam never said those words, and this is actually the first time I've ever "cleaned" on that particular memory. It's not something that I typically would talk about with others. This is something that you do internally, and it changes the energy around you and within you. There might be situations where you actually apologize to someone, but my focus here is on the internal part of the process. For this strategy to work, you need intel, which I've given you the tools to gather. You now know about Freddy—yours and your wife's—and can do reconnaissance, observing the ways he sabotages your relationship (in marriage, for instance, he encouraged me to react in anger to all conflict). With enough intel on Freddy, you can make this cleansing strategy a part of the Target Package that will save your marriage. Instead of reacting in anger when conflict arises, for instance, you can begin your Direct-Action Operations by cleansing.

The deeper you delve into the concepts I have discussed in this chapter, the less foreign they will feel, especially once you try them out yourself. Most Americans are familiar with the precepts of Christianity, even if they didn't grow up in a religious family, and many find things to admire in Jesus's teachings, whether or not they even believe in God. Jesus was all about being tolerant and accepting even the worst people on the planet. He said you shouldn't be judging this woman for committing adultery—not unless you are without sin. This is the same sort of internal exercise I'm encouraging you to practice and make a standard part of your Target Package. Don't focus on looking *outward* at your spouse's faults and mistakes; turn *inward*, and think about your role in what seem to be her flaws.

I remember a time when I was mad at Sam for being complacent. I got very angry with her, but I was oblivious about how her behavior actually reflected mine. Her complacency held a mirror up to my own attitudes. I understood this when I read *Loving What Is* by Byron Katie. Katie's premise is that the universe is basically a big mirror, and of course, nobody reflects your emotional state better than your spouse. So, if your spouse is angry and bitter, judgmental and condemning, that energy is in you, and it needs to be "cleaned" or gotten rid of.

The concept also parallels one of Gandhi's central ideas: be the change you want to see in the world. A successful marriage starts with *you*. We all want to get the Windex out and clean the mirror. We want to make the mirror behave in a way that gets it to reflect what we want. If it doesn't, we get mad at the mirror. Imagine yelling at a mirror for being dirty. Clean yourself, and your inner emotional environment will clean itself.

> Be the change you want to see in the world.

EXECUTION ORDERS

Take responsibility for your life—the good, the bad, and the ugly, and everything in your environment—by empowering your perspective. If you clean yourself up, then your universe will reflect you more clearly. Know that when you get mad at people around you for not acting the way you want them to act, you are yelling at a mirror, and you will get more angry reflections/moments and elicit further anger in your life. If you are calm, cool, and collected in all moments, then you will get a more positive reflection of your life.

CHAPTER 6

CHOOSE HER

Pay attention: this can change your life.

As I said in chapter 2, nothing is more important for a woman than to feel chosen, and her wedding day is her debut of that reality. Women might not openly admit this, but they respond very well to it. We'll get to that in a minute. There is something more important in this "choosing her" discussion that must be addressed first.

In a series of books called *Reality Transurfing*, author Vadim Zeland articulates the most important question people can ask. In fact, they owe it to themselves and the planet to ask and answer this question: What is your definite purpose? Why are you here? This is your most critical question . . . It is absolutely worth doing whatever you need to do to arrive at the right answer for you.

I believe that on the planet today, a majority of the population is not doing what they want most in life. If somebody came up and said, "Did you think you were going to be stacking boxes or digging ditches for your whole life; is that what you chose to do? If you had $350 million right now, is this what you would be doing?" The answer, in almost every instance, would be *no.*

Very few people I have interviewed, as I traveled the world, ever argued that they were doing what they were truly meant to do. Most of them told me that if they could, they would get out immediately. "I would be a writer," they say. "An actor. I would go travel. I would be a pilot." Often, they lament, "I would rather do damn near anything than what I'm doing right now."

Another self-help writer, Napolean Hill, said essentially the same thing as Zeland back in 1937, with *Think and Grow Rich*, a seminal work that the entire self-help industry followed. Another of his books, *Outwitting the Devil*, was written in 1938 but not published until 2011 because of its controversial ideas about religion, education, and parenting. In this work, Hill holds an interview with the devil. Over and over in the book, Hill somehow forces a confession out of the devil. Repeatedly, he asks, "What is the most effective way that people can make sure that you do not control their lives?" The devil always confesses, "Have a definite purpose. Find your definite purpose, and think about nothing else. Fulfill your purpose, think about it, and do only that."

This strategy of focusing on your purpose, according to the book, blocks all avenues for the devil to come into your life to get you to drift. He loves that word: *drift.* There are a slew of things that Freddy will use to encourage you to drift. He will show you things that promise immediate gratification. For certain, he will not show you the consequences of his plans. He promises you the reward and then gives you a plate of garbage. He does it consistently, and he's quite good at it.

Why am I discussing this in a book about marriage? Well, if fulfilling your definite purpose is the most important thing in life and if you are not following your definite purpose with respect to your wife, this is a major source of unhappiness, with all sorts of repercussions, especially for marriage. Before we explore the direct connections to marriage, I'll share some personal examples to demonstrate this concept.

Like many of you, my first experience with people not following their purpose came in my family. My dad, for instance, wanted to be a cop or a test pilot, but he wasn't encouraged in his dreams. My mom wanted to be a psychologist, but she didn't follow through on that goal. My parents both worked for the phone company, and my dad also worked for the military. My sister works for the phone company, too—and no, that wasn't her lifelong dream, either. She wanted to be a doctor.

I joined the military, just like my dad, even though I always wanted to be a pilot. I have pictures of myself building airplanes as a kid. My favorite video games growing up involved flying spaceships. I have fond, fond memories of building cockpits and just sitting in the yard—moving nowhere, of course, but looking at dials that I had drawn on the wood. Those moments were really important to me, yet no one close to me noticed enough to say, "Do you actually want to do this for a living? Here's the kind of living you could have." A nudge like that would have inspired me to follow my dream.

I couldn't stand school and ended up cheating my way through. When the Coast Guard Academy wanted me on the strength of my swimming, I took an entrance exam and scored so poorly in math that I was denied. I enrolled in another school for aviation, but they told me that I was going to have to take two math courses to be allowed into the flight program. I was way behind the power curve.

This was in 1991, when the first Gulf War was underway, and I decided that I needed to do something noble to redeem myself or prove myself worthy. I joined the navy to become a SEAL. Note that these are not words of passion. I'm not saying, "I wanted to be a Navy SEAL more than anything else on planet Earth." I passed my purpose by and did something that was honorable and noble, but I definitely didn't follow my reason for being.

Another way to think of the situation is that I was not listening to my soul. In his *Reality Transurfing* books, Vadim Zeland breaks the person down into a mind and a soul. He adopts an interesting convention in talking about these parts of our being. He substitutes the word "she" for soul and "he" for mind. We have a perception of the soul as a more delicate and refined thing, a kite that wants to fly high in the air, bright and beautiful . . . somehow feminine. The mind needs time to analyze. It's more practical, self-conscious, and deliberative. Often, the soul says, *I want that thing over there*, but the mind says, *No, bad things might happen if we do that. We'll do this safer thing instead.* The soul, which is playful and joyful, wants to achieve your dreams and follow your true purpose. The soul is a kite on a string. She can't force the mind to do anything, but she becomes unhappy and unfulfilled when her desires aren't met.

Sometimes a man does follow his soul. He has a gut feeling about something and needs to do it, perhaps without even knowing why. He might be terrified, but he does it anyway and finds success. When this happens, you arrive at the place where, Zeland says, your soul is "dancing with glee" and your mind is "rubbing his hands with satisfaction." This is what occurs when you pursue the thing that you were meant to do in this life.

So, imagine what you would do with your life if you had $350 million. Whatever the answer, imagine living that kind of life. If you focus on that dream long enough, ideas will blossom to help you get where you want to go. You don't need the $350 million—it's a psychological trick. In *thinking* you have the means to pursue your purpose, something magical happens—a door opens that permits you to go in the right direction. You no longer worry about money, so you can follow your heart's desire.

Why aren't more people headed in the right direction, pursuing their purpose, listening to their soul? The answer is simple: they are at war with their Freddy. You are a thinking being. There is another thinker inside you who is diametrically opposed to everything that you want. We can't hate this thing—but we must understand Freddy's place in our lives so we can move toward what we really want. Freddy can keep you from lining up the various elements of your life if he can get you to drift from your definite purpose.

Mostly we have talked about collecting High-Resolution Intelligence on your spouse and your marriage in order to assemble a Target Package and take Direct-Action Operations to save the relationship, but you must also collect intel on yourself. Discover who you are and what your soul wants, and make focusing on this purpose a part of your Target Package. Any Actions-On Plan should include doing right by yourself as well as by your wife. In fact, these goals are the same.

ACTIONS-ON PLAN

You must choose her. You must choose your soul.

By now, you might be saying, I don't like what Darek is saying. I don't like these metaphors and analogies or the idea that I'm sharing my body with Freddy Kruger. This is fine—we all come to realizations in our own way, with language that makes us comfortable. Forget about any part of this that might rub you the wrong way, and focus on the central questions. Are you happy? Are you following your true purpose? Do you need to reflect and perhaps refocus parts of your life?

These are not idle questions, and they don't touch only on *your* happiness. The title of this chapter is "Choose Her," but so far, we've only talked about your happiness because choosing her is really about choosing your soul. If you are doing the thing that you want to most in life, then that can be very attractive to a woman. She is also supposed to be doing something on this planet that makes her soul dance with glee and her mind rub its hands with satisfaction. If you are both living that kind of life, free and following your dreams, it will be a great example for your children.

Consider what would happen if your attitude were always: *My life is fantastic. I have the woman that I love next to me. My family is next to me. I have the work I've always wanted.* Imagine the energy this creates around you. Other people would begin to think, *I want what he's got.* Your wife will think, *He's happy as can be. What can make me happy? He's asking if I want to try doing various things, and he's supportive.* Imagine how powerful that could be.

This is why choosing her is also about choosing you, choosing your own soul. When you do that, you're choosing to be good to yourself, and you're choosing to take a path that will be an example of how you want your kids to live out their lives. By arriving at your true purpose, you are an inspiration encouraging your wife to find and fulfill her purpose as well. "Choosing her" is the primary reason that marriages succeed, and guys who never learn how to choose their wives are destined to watch their marriages crumble.

This does not mean that you have to have the same purpose as your wife or even that your purposes must be compatible. What if your purposes seem to be in opposition or you're in a situation where you think your wife will never support your purpose? I highly recommend taking some time with this and figuring out who you are and who she is and creating an atmosphere similar to the one that likely existed when you first met her. Remember the time when you talked about all the dreams that you wanted to follow and all of the fun things that you wanted to do? Remind her of the romantic excursions she wanted to take and the things that were going to happen for her. Allow some of those things to happen, and then see what the universe presents. There are probably options that you never thought were possible.

DIRECT-ACTION OPERATIONS

Try some of the strategies articulated in this book. Unless there is physical abuse, now is definitely *not* the time to walk out on your relationship. After reflection and effort, a genuine exploration of possible options, very few men find themselves saying that the *only* way they can pursue their purpose is by severing ties with their wife.

It is vital to figure out who she is while you're exploring your own needs and purpose. For help with learning how to choose your wife, I strongly recommend a book called *His Needs, Her Needs* by Willard Harley. In the book, Harley describes how women want their men to be honest and open. They want financial support and family commitment. These things aren't necessarily the most vital to all guys, but any man who focuses on them for his girl is going to impress her.

She will see and appreciate his effort. (For women reading this book, Harley says men's needs lean toward sexual fulfillment and a regular recreational companion. They want an attractive spouse, domestic support, and admiration.)

A lady friend of mine read *His Needs, Her Needs*, and when she got through the segments on being a recreational companion and an attractive spouse, and depending on men for emotional and financial security, she remarked that these are not concepts many women want to hear, but that if a girl is honest with herself and can accept the message, these ideas will make a major difference in her own happiness. Harley's book contains many helpful tools and resources. The book also contains insight into just about every recreational activity that you can imagine. Couples go through the list and score each activity on a scale of one to ten. The author's recommendation is that a couple only does things together that are a ten on both their lists. If it isn't a ten for both, then it doesn't happen. This means that on Sunday, if football is a ten on his list and a one on hers, the TV stays off.

This does not mean, guys, that you can never watch football again. If she's busy on Monday nights, doing her own thing, of course you can catch a game. The point is that your wife wants *quality* time with you, and that's how you choose her. Give her that quality time. This must be a priority for your marriage. If instead of watching Sunday football, you're out doing something that's a ten on both your lists, then you're choosing her. You both need to work at the plan and stick to it in a spirit of harmony, and this needs to be a part of your Target Package for saving the marriage. You can start

> The point is that your wife wants *quality* time with you, and that's how you choose her. Give her that quality time.

to make these choices on your own—turn off the TV, suggest that walk or movie or whatever she enjoys—as part of your Direct-Action Operations. This is how you keep your marriage instead of losing it to divorce. If you don't choose her, that's it for your marriage.

Often, a surprising and welcome result is that she will choose you in return. You might just find that she wants to watch football on a Sunday, simply enjoying the time with you. It isn't all about negating your desires but rather subsuming those desires on her behalf sometimes.

As you embark on this journey of trying to get things right for her, know in your heart that you're doing the right thing. I want you to consider putting an actual plan together. Look, this marriage thing is no joke—it's way harder than anything I had to do as a Navy SEAL. Marriage is like emotional SEAL training, which is why we're approaching it like a military operation—with Intel, a Target Package, and Direct-Action Operations. You might need help with this strategy, which is one of the reasons for the separate mentorship and coaching I offer (www.sealtohealyourmarriage.com/coach). This book could provide all the focus you need, and that would be great. But if you need help with your plan, then work through these issues with someone you can trust.

RECONNAISSANCE

Let's return to the seven phases of a woman returning to her mate, the Life Discoveries, Inc. pattern I first mentioned way back in chapter 1. As you continue your Direct-Action Operations to choose her, you should do your utmost to meet your wife's needs through all of her phases, however long they take. Being against anything and specifically against things going "too slowly" is the enemy of rebuilding a marriage. Men who begin taking the advice offered here want to see immediate results. They want intimacy, fun, great sex, rewards, and all sorts of benefits as soon as their behavior begins to change. They want to jump to a more advanced phase of the relationship. That's not likely to happen as quickly as you want, but with perseverance and focus, it will happen. As promised, here are the seven phases that you and your wife will work through until she returns:

1. **I hate who you are**. If things are in such chaos that she hates you, and then you start doing the things she really loves, this is how she will respond. In the very depths of her soul, she'll appreciate the things you're doing, but at this point in time, her own Freddy is extremely active. She's been feeding that Bad Wolf a lot, just as you have. She might be thinking, *I'm now interested in that other guy. I want to be with him, and* **now** *you start knocking it out of the park for me? I hate you!* Men, you simply have to stick to the plan, the Target Package, and know in your heart that you're doing the right things.

2. **Civility**. In this phase, she notices what you're becoming and thinks, *Good for you, but I'm still leaving.* There is bitterness still but not complete hatred. She's noting improvements, even if she still thinks you're an ass.

3. **Neutrality**. You've been doing everything you can to choose her, working at it for weeks, maybe months. In this phase, you do something nice, and she says something not so loving at all like, "Thank you for that," but in a voice that is completely neutral, without an ounce of feeling behind it. No excitement in her tone, no love, but the words are positive.

4. **Girlfriend behavior**. This is where things start to get more interesting. She might ask if you can help her with something. There's a little hint of flirtation in there. This is a good place for me to emphasize that it is absolutely imperative that you ride out whatever phase she is in. You can think about and look forward to phase 7, but if she's in phase 4, don't push it. For instance, if she's flirting, you can flirt back, but don't attempt to get intimate. It is *way* too early. Wait for her to take it to the next level. Pushing Mission Execution too soon leads to Mission Failure.

5. **Testing**. In this phase, she will test you, often by demanding help at the most inopportune moments. "I need you to come take care of the kids right now." You have work to do, you're far away, and you're supposed to drop everything. If it's humanly possible, put doing what she asks at the top of your list of Direct-Action Operations. She's really asking you to choose her and testing your level of commitment. If you absolutely can't help, refuse gently and apologetically, and try to come to some other arrangement.

6. **Affair behavior**. If you stay the course and make it through the testing phase, you will begin to notice genuine flirtation. She'll ask you to grab lunch or have dinner out or share a drink. Her behavior will start to have intimate overtones, gestures meant to be exciting that let a guy know he could be closing the deal. Your mission is going well; Direct-Action Operations are working.

7. **The wakeup**. In this final phase, your wife literally wakes up one day and realizes, *I would be completely crazy to leave a man like this.* You have your dream life you have

imagined. You have defeated your Freddy. He has become irrelevant, and you have shown your wife that you really do understand her needs. You've proven that her needs are your priority in spite of the way she's been treating you through these phases. Mission Success!

If you are steadfast about showing your wife that you are choosing her and the things that are important to her, that you have a vision for your family, and that you have resolve in your heart and in your head, then the better and faster you will win her back. But stay patient. If you waffle, as I did, success could take longer to achieve.

How long? The typical time could be two years, but this depends on how bad things have gotten before you begin and how committed you are to this process. I am asking you to fully commit now. I'm telling you that it's worth it to commit now because you do not want to sabotage yourself the way I did. If you do sabotage yourself—these things happen—don't beat yourself up, but get back on the horse. Stay focused on the Target, and don't deviate from the mission. Continue Direct-Action Operations. Tell yourself that your kids and your wife—and most importantly, you—are worth any and every effort to arrive at phase 7.

EXECUTION ORDERS

Is your mind rubbing his hands with satisfaction, and is your soul leaping with joy with what you are doing in life? If not, then spend time identifying why not. If you aren't happy with yourself or your life path, then demanding that your wife provide happiness for you is or will soon be greatly resented. As the Oracle said to Neo in *The Matrix*, "Know yourself."

After this awakening happens and you decide you want to keep your family together, learn what equals "happily ever after" for your wife. Learn what choosing her means, and understand this is a daily request of your wife to you. Your learning to choose her will yield results that both of you will appreciate.

CHAPTER 7

EXECUTE THE MISSION

Win the war for your family's happiness.

O n July 27, 2012, I arrived at Horizon Air Services at Chesapeake Airport, in Virginia. It was a warm summer day, with a crosswind of thirteen knots. I paid close attention to the weather that day because after two years of lessons, I was finally taking the test to get my private pilot's license. The examiner testing me was a Southerner in his midfifties—a fit, polished-looking guy who exuded the authority of a skilled pilot.

"Hey, we have the same birthday," he said. He was about twenty years older than me, but as he went through the reams of paperwork, he noticed that both our birthdays were July 1. It was as if Divine Providence had showed up to my check ride, and I felt in that moment, before I even got in the airplane, that I was going to pass.

I walked up to the Cessna 172 I would be flying and conducted my preflight, checking the gas tank, stall horn, ailerons, rudder . . . Everything looked good, so we strapped ourselves into the cockpit, which was warm but not unbearable because it was such a windy day. I taxied down the runway, and as the plane hit fifty-nine knots, it lifted into the air nice and easy. Once you're airborne, the torque of the engine wants to yaw the airplane, tilting it on a vertical axis, so I applied a little bit of right rudder to make sure we were flying straight as we continued to climb.

I called in to let everybody know where we were going and then headed out to do my check ride as part of the licensing requirements. As part of the certification, you have to do various maneuvers: slow flight, stalls, steep turns at forty-five degrees or greater, and make sure that you maintain a certain altitude, airspeed, and heading. You have a little bit of a buffer, and then you have to do some landings. I was nervous but knew that I could do it.

The flying portion of the examination went perfectly. Remember, I was the kid who built model cockpits in my backyard, monitoring fake dials to pretend I was flying. I was the kid who attempted to make parachutes and leaped from our second-floor windows. I was meant to fly, and after many painful detours, here I was, doing what I was meant to do. I was passing a major milestone on the road to fulfilling my purpose.

I wish I could say everything went perfectly, but that wasn't the case. The examiner ran certain scenarios by me while we flew, and I answered a question wrong. "What do you do if you wake up half an hour after takeoff and you don't remember anything but the airplane is still flying?" he asked. Ironically, this question seemed to point directly at my life. For years, my dream of being a pilot had stalled, along with my marriage, and I felt, in a sense, as if I was waking up—in midlife and midflight—to a second chance. "I would get right to the airport," I answered.

Wrong.

The right answer is that you follow the five Cs—confess, climb, conserve, communicate, and comply.

It's easy for panic and denial to set in when you're lost, so the first step is **confess**: admit to yourself and others that you have wandered off course. Pretending otherwise will only amplify the shock you will feel once the truth sets in. Remain calm and check your instruments to see just how far off course you are. You should also **climb** to the maximum safe altitude that your aircraft can fly. This saves fuel and gives you a better vantage for spotting landmarks. **Conserve** fuel to minimize the chances of having to "perform a crash," or emergency landing. Cut down to the most fuel-efficient speed and power that your aircraft can muster as you wait for instructions. You should **communicate** by calling for help. Air-traffic controllers are there to aid you. Make sure your transponder is on, so you show up on radar. The tower must pinpoint your exact location to formulate the course that will put you back on the right path. This only works, however, if you also **comply**. Don't argue with directions from controllers. Remember, you are the one who's lost, and they have the instruments to guide you back. You're not in a position to dispute their vectors and suggested approaches.

> The right answer is that you follow the five Cs—confess, climb, conserve, communicate, and comply.

This is a solid procedure for flying and good advice for getting your marriage and life back on track. If you're following the advice I've offered here—fulfilling your purpose, choosing you, and choosing her—you will change your environment into something positive, even electric. This is when you feel like you're "in the zone." You're "riding the wave." You're "on your game." Pick the cliché of your choice, but we've all had this feeling of doing something that just feels *right*—something that matches our purpose—and realizing that we can do it well. You might have felt it while running cross-country or tutoring children years ago, singing, fixing cars, or offering advice to friends. Whatever that space is for you, it's the magical point when you're finally living life with grace and confidence.

The transition to riding the wave and executing the mission is not immediate. You must collect Intel, formulate a Target Package, and give the Direct-Action Operations your all. This takes work and practice, just as I had years of flying lessons before I got to that liberating day when I took the flight to get certified. There will be points along the way at which you fall asleep, get off course, stall out, or otherwise screw up in midflight—and midmarriage. The important thing in those moments is to remember the five Cs.

Not only did I answer a question wrong on the day of my flight test, but when the examiner asked me to do a "short-field landing," I did not set my manifold pressure correctly, in order to keep our landing speed under seventy-two knots. When we came in, faster than we should have, there was a significant crosswind, too. The combination overwhelmed me, and I bounced down the runway. It was about the worst short-field landing a pilot could imagine.

I finally stopped the plane, and the examiner looked at me as if to say, "What was that?" I felt dejected, thinking I'd failed. I'd done so many good landings, and then I had to go and have my worst one ever during my check ride. We did a couple more runs—circling the airport and coming in for various other types of landings, and finally, I pulled up to the terminal and parked. People were waiting for me to celebrate my getting certified, but I wasn't so sure. Dribbling your airplane down the runway is not something that you want to do with your flight examiner.

The examiner turned to me, expressionless, then smiled. "Congratulations," he said and handed me my pilot's certificate. The emotions welled up, and by the time I called my dad in the car, I was crying tears of joy. *This is awesome*, was all I could think. The dream had finally come true.

That day was key for me in fulfilling my purpose. I've talked about how fulfilling your purpose (in my case, flying) relates to living a life of satisfaction and grace, to "riding the wave." But what does it mean to fulfill your dreams in your marriage? How do you execute the mission to win the war for your family's happiness? In Larry Bilotta's marriage-saving Environment Changer course, he calls the kind of person who achieves Mission Success an "Environment Changer."

You might have experienced this type of person when you met a magnetic celebrity, the kind who is automatically happy you're around them. They emit a positive vibe, and you join them in it for an experience that feels great. Maybe this wasn't a celebrity for you, but a grandmother, teacher, or a new acquaintance. It might be somebody who just shows up in your universe, and you immediately like them.

They look at you and aren't aware of any of the terrible things you might have done or things you're embarrassed about, and you sense immediately that they like you. You sense immediately that they like themselves too. This is the kind of person who, when an ugly situation arises, diffuses the drama in a healthy way. People might remain angry, but this person calms things down and makes the space for a conversation and a solution. To become an Environment Changer in your marriage, you must work through the following five steps:

STEP 1: Identify your definite purpose.

Ask yourself why you are on this planet. If you won the lottery right now, what would you do? Find your definite purpose. Focusing on your true purpose, as Napolean Hill points out, blocks all avenues for the devil to come into your life and forces you to do dumb things that your wife and kids will hate and that will get you to drift off the purpose.

STEP 2: Identify core programming.

These are the deeply held beliefs and attitudes, which you might not even be aware of, that are holding you back in life. You must alter negative core programs in order to replace the troubling brain instructions from your past so that you can focus on your future.

STEP 3: Take 100 percent responsibility—clean the mess.

This is where you engage in the lessons we have learned from the ancient Hawaiian art of ho'oponopono. If a situation is negative, take responsibility for it and clean it, using the methods we've discussed. Remember to internally "clean" the bad stuff by reflecting: I'm sorry. I love you. Please forgive me. Thank you. While you're cleaning, it's important to appreciate the thing that you can be happiest about in the situation, no matter how undesirable the overall scenario.

STEP 4: Execute the mission—ride the wave.

This is when you feel like you're connected, tapped in, tuned in, with it, in the zone, riding the wave . . . You are taking the gray lump of clay you have been given and molding it into something positive and beautiful. You have been calling all things—whether they seem good or bad at first—good, and the tide has turned. You have created the conditions for inspiration to arrive.

Meditation or prayer can help you get to this place. Simply sitting down in comfortable clothes and focusing on your breathing fifteen minutes a day works wonders. When negative thoughts enter your mind, let them drift away. If a positive stream of thought enters your head, realize that it is probably inspiration. Freddy will resist this practice to the point that you won't want to follow through with it. Whether it is mediation or prayer, it can reduce stress and put you in a place where you are in touch with your definite purpose.

STEP 5: Manifest your new energy.

In this phase, you will see things come true that you have been thinking about and imagining. Once you're putting out this sort of energy and seeing positive things happen, nothing is impossible. These might be clichés, but the sky truly is the limit and the world is your oyster.

The work does not end, and the process does not happen in a clean straight line. There will be setbacks. Let's say you are in step

5 and you run into a negative situation you didn't want to happen. At this point, it's important to go back to step 3. Remember and reaffirm that you are responsible for your entire reality. Somehow, someway you created what seems like an "undesirable" situation, but you must not call it "undesirable." Instead, you must mold that clay into something good. Apologize for whatever appears undesirable at first glance, and make it right with ho'oponopono.

You might need to meditate again, to think and talk about what you want, to refocus on your definite purpose. The goal is to get back to the positive energy and positive thought you were creating before. We all get bumped off the wave, but according to the law of attraction, if you focus on the negative, it will bring more negative. Always focus on the positive aspects of any situation. If doing this seems strange to you, you're not alone. Here's a story that illustrates the power of this approach to life:

A monk was being chased by a ferocious tiger. The tiger chased him to the edge of a cliff. He looked back, terrified, and then noticed a vine. He jumped onto the vine, dangling just below the snarling tiger. The monk shimmied down a few feet, but three hundred feet below, jagged rocks rose up like fangs. If he fell, he would be killed on the rocks. Just then, two mice began to gnaw at the vine. Looking from the ferocious tiger above to the jagged rocks below, the monk noticed on the cliff wall, an arm's length away, a cluster of strawberries growing wild. He reached out and plucked one. He bit into it, and it turned out to be the most amazing strawberry he'd ever tasted.

Too often in life, we're focused on the ferocious tiger above and the jagged rocks below, to the point that we believe we have no third choice, but we do! Might as well enjoy the strawberry before we die. Who knows, the tiger might find easier prey close by and leave. The mice might stop chewing the vine. A way of escape might make itself known, so enjoy that delicious strawberry.

HIGH-RESOLUTION INTELLIGENCE

Good decisions on the battlefield and in life have rewards that make the effort worthwhile.

It was a typical mission in Afghanistan. We had intelligence that warranted a kill/capture operation, and Execution Orders were given. You are not going to get specific details about how intelligence was collected or how we arrived on target. Those kinds of things are classified and need to remain that way for national-security reasons. That being said, it is worth providing a snapshot of a piece of that operation to highlight the value of a good decision.

We arrived on target and made entry. I noticed a closed door immediately to my right and an Air Force PJ, a para-rescue specialist, followed me through it. We cleared the room and quickly stacked (made ourselves ready for a forced entry) on the next door. He gave me the squeeze, and we made entry. I double-tapped a guy with an AK-47 and quickly determined the other two MAMs (military age males) in the room were not a threat. After the rest of the compound was cleared, we began SSE (sensitive site exploitation). The two guys I didn't shoot threw up on the floor until they were escorted into another room for tactical questioning.

In the aftermath of that event, we discovered that those two guys who I did not shoot were actually protecting family from the terrorist who had forced them to house and feed him. The family was grateful that the terrorist was dead and even more thankful that they hadn't lost their sons, who were standing next to him when he died. The guy whose life I took that night was a Taliban regional commander, and his loss was a severe blow to that network.

If those boys get hurt, the US gets a black eye because the family would complain of losses they should not have endured. If the Taliban commander doesn't die, more Americans and allies are at risk of attack. Who knows how much effect the operation had, but the point I'm going to make here is this:

Freddy might be fully operational and wielding his worst. If you are hated by your wife, chances are high she thinks you are the Freddy. Ending his reign doesn't mean your removal from the planet. You are, after all, a good man. But when Freddy is neutralized, your family and your wife are happy. Her seeing the man she fell in love with and your kids seeing the loving father and husband you're meant to be are worth the effort of focusing on your best life, which renders Freddy all but dead.

EXECUTION ORDERS

Gathering intel on your marriage and assembling a Target Package like the one we had for the kill/capture operation I described is not easy. Carrying out Direct-Action Operations in your marriage will involve busting down doors every bit as sturdy and ominous as the ones I busted through in that Afghan building—doors that put your needs before hers. The forbidding doors you face are composed not of oak or steel but of destructive programs that are even stronger because they were constructed so long ago you can't even see these doors without serious efforts. Such doors block communication so completely that you and your wife might as well be speaking different languages, and these doors, too, hide a kind of terrorist bent on destroying you and your marriage. Use the tools in this book or in my coaching program to break down the doors.

Once you gain entry, calmly target and take out Freddy. Getting angry and firing wildly won't work. In fact, anger will probably result in the kind of collateral damage that makes a bad situation worse—just as my firing wildly would have taken out that family's innocent sons and damaged our mission. You must stay focused and train your sights only on your highest purpose. This isn't easy, because of the worst part: Freddy has been wearing your face. If you go to court, you are held responsible for his actions. If you get trigger happy and hurt the innocent sons, the family's grief is your fault. If you face your wife and your Freddy comes out, she is not going to be all that interested in reestablishing the family ties that you are longing for right now if she has left you.

By implementing the tools you have here, you will achieve your dream and put smiles on both your and your family's hearts. Your Freddy does not deserve mercy, but your family members do. Having the discernment to "shoot" the terrorist and not your family members is vital to your success. This concept is mind-bending and frankly, harder than anything I've done as a Navy SEAL. How to react to being attacked by the ones you love most requires complete reprogramming. This means identification and removal of old worthless programming and a build-out of *new effective programming*. Start with framing, and then put in new wiring, walls, and doors, and decorate the house as you test out this new program until a full reliable install is complete. As I said, this is harder than anything I've ever done in the SEAL teams, but it requires the same kind of determination and courage as a SEAL mission. The stakes are just as high, and the consequences for delaying or not doing this right are severe. The more heat you can deal with, as soon as possible and in a healthy way, the better the chances are that your marriage will succeed.

CONCLUSION

A GUY WHO'S GETTING IT RIGHT

A friend of mine threw a barbecue for his wife's birthday. He is a conscientious father and husband who has worked hard to create a positive family environment. He did an epic job of celebrating her birthday. The actual day was Sunday, the day after the big barbecue, but he'd been doing birthday stuff for her all weekend. He took multiple days off, went swimming with her, found great gifts, and took on extra duties with the kids. He did a great job making her feel special.

Everything was going great leading up to Sunday night. His avalanche of awesomeness had genuinely touched her. But he didn't know that it was always important for his wife to have a cake and blow out a candle on her actual birthday. This was her family's tradition, as far back into girlhood as she could remember, and it meant a lot to her. All he knew, however, was that on Sunday night she decided to bake a cake.

The cake did not turn out so well, and then their young daughter attempted to put frosting on it and screwed things up further. His wife's mood took a turn south, and she became short with him. From his perspective, he had done everything up until that moment that he could do to make her happy and give her a great birthday, and now she was abusing him because of something he considered trivial.

As her mood worsened, he began to get angry. He'd been resting, sitting down after all the hard work he'd done for her birthday weekend. When his wife asked him to come watch her blow out that candle and he didn't leap up, she became angry with him for not understanding her important family ritual, and he grew furious with her. How could she not appreciate all he'd done to be sensitive to her feelings? Typical male behavior: hurt and on the defensive, we beg for her to understand the long list of things we do (speaking German the whole time). We want our wives to go back to being fun and flirtatious, while praising all our great deeds. But in an argument, a list just tells a wife that he is not listening to her, that he is only focused on what he has accomplished, not on her wishes, needs, and desires. He began making a deal with his Freddy, who urged my friend, "Hey, get really angry at her. Let her know what a jerk she is for not being sensitive to your feelings."

In that moment, each of their Freddies was working hard to destroy all of the good that happened over the weekend. My friend wanted his wife to admit that she was being insensitive to him and his avalanche of awesomeness that he had accomplished for her birthday weekend. While for her, even though she knew that he'd done many wonderful things, she wasn't mad about the weekend. She was angry with him for not making that particular moment joyful for her. The moment is the thing that matters. So, as often happens, the wife in the relationship went into manage-the-angry-man-mode. While she needed him to not get upset, he, a Precise person (which requires others to be sensitive to their feelings), ignored all that and instead got caught up in her sour reaction to the candle incident.

He accidentally and unwittingly blamed her just like I blamed Sam for not seeing how hard I worked on things. In the same way, so many men in troubled marriages blame their wives without meaning harm but causing harm anyway. He looked at the situation through the lens that made the most sense to him. That's why he wound up attempting to force her to understand that he was right.

After an operation, SEALs go back to the drawing board and conduct a "hot wash," during which they review the entire operation. The long knives come out, and if anything went wrong, we address it, usually with passion, because we're professionals who want to keep ourselves and our brothers alive—and it's fun to get things right. My friend reacted like a complete Navy SEAL in the "hot wash" of what happened over the birthday weekend. Unfortunately, that is not how you should conduct business with most human beings, certainly not in marriage. He treated his wife as *he* would want to be treated after an operation, not as *she* wanted to be treated. He was not programmed to understand that making the relationship successful (and accepting how she acts) is the priority, not analyzing why she is wrong. He would have been better served by taking 100 percent responsibility for the mess and then trying a totally different approach, keeping things light, flirtatious, joking, and fun—because this was what she wanted.

So, how might this scenario have gone better? For starters, if my friend had been aware of the anger drug being offered to him, then he could have eliminated it simply by molding the gray clay into something positive and beautiful and calling the thing good. He could have realized that his wife, a Joyful person, is not driven by sensitivity to other people's feelings the way he is. She wasn't about to count off a list of the things he had done right for her. Instead, she was looking at the present moment (especially important for a Joyful person). For him to accept whatever she does is more important to her than his list of achievements in almost all circumstances, and is very different from what he values.

While he didn't see her perspective in that moment, his avalanche of awesomeness over that birthday weekend did help him tremendously to avoid a relationship disaster. On top of that, any high-level awareness in that moment could have made things *even better* than either of them ever imagined, simply by him shifting his perspective. If he had understood how delighted his wife is when, no matter what she does, he just completely accepts however she acts, then he would have hit a grand slam. (Especially since forgiving and forgetting mean everything to a Joyful person.) In that case, the moment would have went something like, "I didn't know about the candle tradition that's so special to you. My back is killing me right now, but let's see what we can do." What if he'd then gone upstairs, brought the kids down, and lit a special candle for her? What if he'd turned the event into a surprise? He might have saved the moment. This night could have become a great memory for both of them. This reimagining redeems that moment and transforms the energy of that moment into a much better feeling. It allows for forgiveness and for everyone involved to feel relieved that the situation has been made right—Ho'oponopono style: I'm sorry. I love you. Please forgive me. Thank you. The key realization is that his acceptance of what she does is more important to her than his requirement for others to be sensitive to another's feelings. That awareness is high-level relationship operations. And that is where you are going with your wife.

When you try hard to make somebody else happy so that you can be happy, you'll always fail yourself. If your happiness depends on your wife treating you well, then no matter what your wife's emotional condition, you are handing her the power to decide how you will feel. Programming played into this situation as well. How did my friend's mom and dad treat him? What happened in his childhood home? Did they yell at him because he wasn't doing things to make them feel good? Does he need his wife's validation because he didn't get enough validation from his parents?

Understanding his childhood programs might have helped my friend step back, assess the situation, and choose the better path. Gathering High-Resolution Intelligence on himself and his wife would have allowed him to assemble a detailed Target Package and then engage in the Direct-Action Operations that could lower tension and change the dynamics. Is he aware of his own childhood programs? Did his wife's parents divorce when she was a child? One of the things that his wife remembered growing up was being able to blow a candle out on her birthday. Is it possible that her programming comes from wanting her father to be there for her, even though he never was as much as she wanted him to be? If that's the case, her husband might come through for her on many fronts, but failure on that one important front can still trigger the hurt that she took on as a program as a little girl, a program that causes her to react emotionally as an adult today. Did her programmed emotional reaction trigger his programming of not feeling valued when he was growing up? I would bet this is exactly what happened.

Despite that one moment, my friend's avalanche of awesomeness toward his wife was very much noticed and very much appreciated. In writing to me the story of the candle incident, my friend's wife included a reflection. "I just needed to be sensitive to all the things he had done and consider that he might have been tired and in pain when I asked him if he wanted to join in. He then would have joined us happily! I was just getting so frustrated with myself that I could not see anyone else. If I would have been positive, happy and confident, the whole situation would have been positive as well!"

There you go, gentlemen! The avalanche of awesomeness that my friend invested in by constantly showing his wife how much he adores and cherishes her is everything. Tons of emotional money in her emotional bank means she'll consider another perspective other than the one her Freddy wants to give her to ruin the whole damn thing. My friend struck out in that moment but he hit so many home runs over the weekend. She knows he wants to make things fun for her. He got enough right for her that this event ultimately turned out to be a great learning moment in their relationship. I'm so proud and happy for them. He's a man who's working through it and despite the momentary setback, he is getting it right. And he will only get better!

Throughout this book, we've discussed scenarios like this one, in which people intend the good thing but end up doing exactly the wrong thing. They don't understand themselves. They don't understand why their relationship is not working, and it becomes a disaster. Most people go through life living out this disaster. They see their marriage options as (1) endure the disaster, (2) accept that nothing will ever change, (3) stay married and miserable, or (4) decide they can't live this way and divorce.

In all these scenarios, partners simply want to enjoy a fulfilling life. They might try self-help books and counseling. Those might provide some insights, but they generally don't succeed (marriage counseling rarely works because counselors focus on behavior instead of creating acceptance and appreciation in the couple).

My approach has been to help men wake up to the reality that they are unique—and so are their wives. Without understanding, acceptance, and appreciation of the most important people in your life—you, her, your kids—you can't live by the real Golden Rule, which is to treat others as they wish to be treated. You will be well served by making an effort to understand her attitudes and to realize that you and she see the world through very different lenses. You would be wise to note these patterns, collect intel on them, and appreciate that most of your attitudes toward marriage were formed by age ten, so changing your negative childhood programs takes focus.

You shouldn't fixate on your Freddy, but identifying him and naming him is key. Understand that you want a family that is close, safe, and protected—and that your Freddy doesn't want that. You now have the means to turn your Freddy into a helpful reminder. Yes, you can make him a kind of assistant, a constant reminder to do the opposite of what he wants you to do.

More important, you now know that you can transform your relationship with your wife through self-reflection and the process of "taking 100 percent responsibility and cleaning the mess." Using the tools in this book, you know how to pull things from your subconscious and understand that if they are in your world, then you are in some way responsible for them. And if they're here, then you can heal the pain they've caused. You can take Direct-Action Operations based on that intel.

Choosing your soul is vital. Your soul loves you, your wife, and your family, so getting it right for them means getting it right for yourself—and then staying in that zone where you will experience the relationship you planned. There is nothing sweeter than living in the zone, riding the wave, and allowing flow into your life. This is how you create a better relationship, career, finances, or whatever it is that you want to create. You now realize that getting angry with those you love because they are not behaving the way you want is perhaps the most obvious mistake.

I made that mistake for years, along with plenty of others, and I hope that, in writing this book, I can help other men get back on track and avoid those same mistakes before it's too late. My marriage with Sam ended, and I'm still repairing the damage. You can benefit from my discoveries and all of the work and insight that came out of the real causes of my failed marriage.

I retired from the SEAL teams after twenty-four years to follow my purpose: flying as a certified pilot. I also am using my experiences and hard-won knowledge to serve men as a marriage and life coach. I am speaking and writing to reach men in troubled relationships in order to help them keep their families together—perhaps my highest purpose. In short, I am riding the wave, in the zone. I have found the path to a life of grace and mercy, acceptance and gratitude—and it is giving me great satisfaction. I hope this book helps you to live such a life as well.

A FINAL NOTE FROM THE AUTHOR

WHAT NOW?

I'm going to assume that you read my book and have taken it to heart. I'm also going to assume that the things I have explained have real meaning for you and that you are sincerely interested in changing the direction of your life—not just for your wife but for yourself, too. If that's the case, then you and I have a lot in common. I was exactly where you are when I reached out to Larry Bilotta for help years ago.

I want your pain to be temporary because, although pain can wake you and shake you, if it remains without resolution, you can end up becoming somebody you're really not. It's my intention to help you be yourself. That's the most important mission on earth. The problem is that we don't really know ourselves. We might know what we feel as we are tossed around on a sea of emotions, but we don't know who we really are.

Knowing who you are matters because that's how you get to your mission in life. A woman admires and follows a man who knows who he is and knows what he wants. Confused and selfish men are a turnoff. If you are looking for my help, this is the kind of help I'm going to give you.

There are really five kinds of guys I work with, and these five could benefit by applying my process. Read these descriptions, and see which guy you might be.

BULL IN A CHINA SHOP

The Bull in the China Shop does not know he's in a china shop. He has all the answers, and his wife has complained often that he does not listen.

I was the Bull in the China Shop. I had no idea what my wife, or even my children, needed. You are the Bull in the China Shop if your opinion is the only one that matters.

NO-CONFLICT MAN

The No-Conflict Man does anything and everything to stay away from confrontation. He is an Easygoing guy who works to create efficiency so he can relax. Even though he works for peace, he does not find it very often. That's because his biggest offense in his wife's eyes is that when she wants him to "fight back" to show that he cares, No-Conflict Man simply shuts down and stops talking. This drives her crazy, to the point that an Easygoing man does not get the respect he wants. You are a No-Conflict Man if you've heard your wife get frustrated about you shutting down and not sharing your true feelings.

DEEP THINKER SCIENTIST

The Deep Thinker Scientist is a Precise guy. He is analytical in almost every situation because he's looking for a deep analytical perspective on why people do what they do. The Deep Thinker Scientist gets upset when his wife does not care about what he just knows is the right thing to care about. He gets angry with her when she's insensitive to his emotional condition.

MOVIN' ON MAN

The Movin' On Man is usually a Joyful guy. He wants to be accepted for what he does, and since his wife doesn't meet that need, he can easily decide to move on once he decides she's not making him feel good anymore. He might have tried to do things that made her happy, but when he did not get the expected praise, he felt let down. Movin' On Man can easily see a difficult relationship situation as "impossible" when it does not get better quickly on its own.

SAD, SENSITIVE, GUILTY MAN

The Sad, Sensitive, Guilty Man could be a Precise guy but might also have any of the personalities. He is very aware that he screwed up badly, especially if this is not the first marriage he has broken. He's full of sorrow about what he has lost. He's painfully sensitive to all that's happened, and he revisits those memories often. He's paying a high price for reliving his guilt. Being remorseful because you're taking responsibility will help slow down your negative energy, but if that guilty burden isn't lifted soon, you will become a tortured soul. If you are the Sad, Sensitive, Guilty Man, you make it difficult for your wife to be near you. She is initially glad that you feel bad, but she wants you to get back to normal. If you stay too down for too long, you'll turn into a needy guy she does not want to prop up.

If this book has helped but you need more guidance to find yourself and save your marriage, I also work directly with men to do just that. I take them through the same process that allowed me to change and to create and maintain healthy relationships. This process has five phases. Each phase moves you closer to the goal of knowing yourself and knowing what you truly want in life.

You might say, "But Darek, how can you help me get my wife to love me again?" To that I would say, "You are asking the wrong question. Your wife stopped loving you for a set of reasons that you are just beginning to understand. When you look at the five kinds of men and relate to one or more of them, you are looking at the reasons why your wife can justify rejecting you. Instead, you need to become the kind of man your wife *wants* to pursue.

These are the five phases I will help you through:

Phase 1:
Learn what motivates you and how you were programmed.

Phase 2:
Learn how to shut off that little voice inside your head
that creates your negative emotions.

Phase 3:
Learn where self-confidence and happiness really originate,
and then create them in yourself.

Phase 4:
Build your positive momentum, and gain the ability to
create the situations you want.

Phase 5:
Live as the man she wants to be with.

Two free videos available on my website
(www.sealtohealyourmarriage.com/coach)
will get you started and explain in more detail how I work with
men who decide to use my coaching services.

EXECUTION ORDERS

Mind your thoughts, they become your words.
Mind your words, they become your actions.
Mind your actions, they become your habits.
Mind your habits, they become your character.
Mind your character, it becomes your destiny.

AFTERWORD

People who read my first draft wanted to know what happened to Sam and if she'd also done some things that might be considered not so nice. I will address those questions here.

I officially married Sam in San Diego in 1998 to meet immigration requirements that would allow her to stay with me. It became clear then that our relationship would be hard on both of us, and it almost ended at least one time. The family wedding happened in Australia several months later. Sam had dated a guy a long time before she met me, and he was a guest at our wedding. I have actually always liked this guy a lot and still do. At some point I noticed him looking at Sam, and I could see immediately that he loved her in the way that all girls want to be loved, a way that I knew I didn't feel toward her. If I hadn't already been married to her, I would have walked up to him and said, "Hey, man, it's clear you wish you had another chance here. Do you want her? Because I can tell from the look you just gave her that I obviously don't love her the way you do."

I, of course, did not say that. Sam and I stayed married and ended up having kids. That doesn't make a troubled marriage any easier. When Sam went back to Australia with the kids, that old boyfriend was, of course, the guy who started coming around, and now, years later, he has the love of his life. He's married to Sam and is no doubt doing a bang-up job raising our kids as best he can with Sam. I'm happy that true love made that situation happen for them. I truly am. I miss my kids, and I miss talking to Sam, but if I'm completely honest here, my programming would have made a greater mess of their lives. The kids are better off living with Sam and her new husband. It has taken me a long time to arrive at a place in my heart where I realize this and that somehow, my kids and future generations will be more blessed because of everything that has happened. My not getting the kids back resulted in eight years of suffering, but that pain and reflection gave me the insight to help other families get it right. I believe the tragedy of my divorce happened because I'm supposed to pass these lessons on to you.

Early readers also wanted me to acknowledge that I'm a good guy and that despite my inadequacies as a father and husband, I tried my best. They figured Sam must have played a part in making the marriage and breakup harder than it needed to be. I validate these ideas without patting myself on the back or throwing Sam under the bus. But I was completely clueless. Of course, Sam didn't appreciate having to deal with ten years of my bullshit. Of course, she resented me with just cause, and of course, I endured the kinds of consequences that many divorced men justifiably rage against. I chose not to. I arrived at a place in my heart where I knew that harboring the smallest amount of contempt for her or for anyone was not healthy. I didn't like being perpetually angry. It was exhausting.

I took 100 percent responsibility for causing this whole nightmare—and doing that has allowed marriage partners across the country to reconcile without having to endure the brutal losses I did. I tell all of them to thank Sam for beating me to within an inch of my life and leaving me for dead so that I could articulate, in no uncertain terms, to readers like you that it is totally worth it to do things differently than I did. Showing your family you care about them is truly caring for their well-being and yours.

As I end, I want to take this opportunity to say a couple things to Sam and my children.

I am sorry I was a terrible husband and father. Please take this book to all mankind as an apology of the highest order for any and all hurt you harbor because of how badly I failed you. I love you all very much.

—Darek/Dad

APPENDIX: RESOURCES

WEB

- Life Discoveries, Inc., www.YouCanSaveThisMarriage. com: online courses developed by Larry Bilotta (The Environment Changer Program, Softhearted Woman Hard World, Marriage 101, Survive a Midlife Crisis, The Flag Page Tool)

BOOKS

- *The Physics of Miracles*, Richard Bartlett and Melissa Joy Johnson

- *The 5 Love Languages*, Gary Chapman

- *The Hidden Messages in Water*, Masaru Emoto

- *His Needs, Her Needs: Building an Affair-Proof Marriage*, Willard F. Harly, Jr.

- *Getting into the Vortex: Guided Meditations CD and User's Guide*, Esther and Jerry Hicks

- *Money and the Law of Attraction: Learning to Attract Wealth, Health, and Happiness*, Esther and Jerry Hicks

- *The Vortex: Where the Law of Attraction Assembles All Cooperative Relationships*, Esther and Jerry Hicks

- *Think and Grow Rich,* Napoleon Hill and Arthur R. Pell

- *Outwitting the Devil: The Secret to Freedom and Success,* Napoleon Hill and Sharon L. Lechter

- *Loving What Is: Four Questions That Can Change Your Life,* Byron Katie

- *The Love Dare,* Alex and Stephen Kendrick

- *Between Two Worlds: The Inner Lives of Children of Divorce,* Elizabeth Marquardt

- *Busting Loose from the Money Game: Mind-Blowing Strategies for Changing the Rules of a Game You Can't Win,* Robert Schienfield

- *Zero Limits: The Secret Hawaiian System for Wealth, Health, Peace, and More,* Joe Vitale and Ihaleakala Hew Len

- *At Zero: The Final Secrets to "Zero Limits" the Quest for Miracles through Ho'oponopono,* Joe Vitale

- *Reality Transurfing,* Vadim Zeland

FILM

- *The Matrix* series, directed by Andy and Lana Wachowski

- *What the Bleep Do We Know!?,* directed by William Arntz, Betsy Chasse, and Mark Vicente

Printed in the USA
CPSIA information can be obtained
at www.ICGtesting.com
JSHW012052140824
68134JS00035B/3399

9 781599 326924